James Joyce's *Ulysses*

James Joyce's

Ulysses

A Book of Many Happy Returns

Brook Thomas

Louisiana State University Press
Baton Rouge and London

Designer: Rod Parker
Typeface: Gill Sans
Typesetter: G & S Typesetters, Inc.
Printer: Thomson-Shore
Binder: Thomson-Shore

Quotations from *Ulysses*, by James Joyce (copyright 1914, 1918 by
Margaret Caroline Anderson and renewed 1942, 1946 by Nora
Joseph Joyce), are reprinted by permission of Random House, Inc.,
The Bodley Head Limited, and the Society of Authors as the literary
representative of the Estate of James Joyce.

Library of Congress Cataloging in Publication Data

Thomas, Brook.
    James Joyce's Ulysses.

    Includes index.
    I. Joyce, James, 1882–1941.   Ulysses.   I. Title.
PR6019.09U74   1982   823'.912   82-7809
ISBN 0-8071-1044-2   AACR2

For my parents, who made returning a pleasure

"Years dreams return"   (*U* 382.17)

Contents

Abbreviations

CW	Joyce, James. *The Critical Writings of James Joyce*, ed. Ellsworth Mason and Richard Ellmann. New York: Viking Press, 1959.
Dubliners	Joyce, James. *"Dubliners": Text, Criticism and Notes*, ed. Robert Scholes and A. Walton Litz. New York: Viking Press, 1969.
JJ	Ellmann, Richard. *James Joyce*. New York: Oxford University Press, 1959.
Letters, I, II, III	Joyce, James. *Letters of James Joyce*. Vol. I, ed. Stuart Gilbert. New York: Viking Press, 1957; reissued with corrections, 1965. Vols. II and III, ed. Richard Ellmann. New York: Viking Press, 1966.
P	Joyce, James. *A Portrait of the Artist as a Young Man*. The definitive text corrected from the Dublin Holograph by Chester G. Anderson and edited by Richard Ellmann. New York: Viking Press, 1964.
U	Joyce, James. *Ulysses*. New York: Random House, 1934; reset and corrected, 1961. References are to page and line numbers.

Acknowledgments

I wrote this book sitting at borrowed desks and kitchen tables from Honolulu to Budapest. I thank all those who were my hosts and who gave support. Institutional support came from the literature department of the University of Constance in the Federal Republic of Germany, which allowed a young, unknown American to teach an advanced seminar on Joyce and which later provided the proper atmosphere for me to continue research while financed by a grant from the Alexander von Humboldt-Stiftung.

Permission to quote from *Ulysses* has been granted by Random House, The Bodley Head Limited, and The Society of Authors, London. Chapter Five is a revised version of an essay that first appeared in *Genre* and is adapted from my essay in *The Seventh of Joyce*, edited by Bernard Benstock, copyright © 1982 by Indiana University Press, and reprinted with the permission of the publisher. I have also incorporated material that I used previously in three essays in the *James Joyce Quarterly*, an essay in *Modern British Literature*, and an essay commissioned by *Editions de L'Herne*, Paris.

If I have learned anything in preparing this study, which is in part about the act of reading *Ulysses*, it is that all readings of *Ulysses* necessarily depend on the work of readers who have come before, even those readers with whom one disagrees. The community of readers generated by Joyce's texts is much more than an "industry" and deserves my thanks. Three fellow readers merit special mention. Through his example, Hugh Kenner showed me the attention Joyce's texts demand and the rewards to be gained from paying them that attention. Herbert N. Schneidau read and reread early versions so often that, if my argument in Chapter Five has any truth, he must be considered my partner (the more accomplished one) in rewriting. Finally, Fritz Senn made available his library, his notes, his apartment, and the most flexible and reflexive mind reading Joyce's language that we have. Thus, while I must take responsibility for having arranged this particular argument, I find it hard to call what follows "my" reading.

James Joyce's *Ulysses*

Introduction

Good Idea the Repetition

Let me start by explaining my title. By calling *Ulysses* a book of "many happy returns" (*U* 93.12–13), I most obviously allude to the fact that *Ulysses* is Joyce's birthday book, appearing as it did on his fortieth birthday: 2 February 1922. Less apparent is my allusion to one of the best short pieces ever written on *Ulysses*, Fritz Senn's "Book of Many Turns."[1] Senn's emphasis on the polytropic nature of *Ulysses*—he uses Homer's description of Odysseus, *polytropos*—has confirmed and influenced the way I think about *Ulysses*. What I try to do is to emphasize that the book's many turns also involve many returns.

In writing his own version of Homer's epic, Joyce borrows the Odyssean return story pattern, a pattern that structures the wanderings of character Leopold Bloom through Dublin, 16 June 1904. Bloom, however, is not the only one to trace an odyssey of return in the book. In writing his book of many happy returns, Joyce himself traces an odyssey of a disappearing and returning artist. Furthermore, the reader finds himself playing the role of Odysseus as he steers his way through the book's pages. In a letter to Harriet Shaw Weaver, 25 February 1920, Joyce reveals that he considers both his writing of the book and the reading of it as odysseys. "I am working now on 'Oxen of the Sun' the most difficult episode in an odyssey, I think, both

1. Fritz Senn, "Book of Many Turns," *James Joyce Quarterly*, X (Fall, 1972), 29–46.

1

to interpret and to execute" (*Letters, I* 137).[2] Indeed, Joyce's relationship to the reader is similar to that between the gods and Odysseus. Just as the gods both aid and hinder Odysseus in his return voyage to Ithaca, so artist-god Joyce places stylistic barriers in the reader's way and then helps the reader navigate by self-consciously commenting on how those barriers were created.

Mention of those self-conscious comments brings me to one more return I will consider, that is, how the book turns back on itself, making *Ulysses* one of the foremost examples of a reflexive work of literature.

In my emphasis on *Ulysses* as a book of many happy returns, I will adopt that simple and very Joycean method of exhausting the possibilities of a metaphor as an organizing principle. The choice of my particular metaphor calls for me continually to return to parts of *Ulysses*, examining them from different perspectives and in different contexts. I will not apologize for this method, because I feel that this technique of repetition is called for by the nature of the book. If this method leads to an awareness of the limitations of return as a metaphor for reading, that does not invalidate its usefulness as an aid in reading the book; returns imply perpetually new turns, what we weave often gets unwoven.

Before setting keel to breakers to depart on my odyssey through the book, I want to spend considerable time clarifying my position on a number of critical questions that my study raises and distinguishing my position from those of others writing on Joyce. If an introduction devoted largely to previous criticism seems a bit tedious, it will end with a return to the text, and it should provide clearer sailing later on. Furthermore, since a major concern of mine is how we read *Ulysses'* polytropic language, earlier criticism provides me with examples I need of readers reading.

Two terms that I will use throughout should be clarified from the start: *self-consciousness* and *reflexivity*. The distinction between them is important. When I use the word *self-consciousness* it refers to a state of mind. We can have a self-conscious writer, one continuously

2. See also *Letters, I* 129, 147, 163; *Letters, II* 465.

aware that he is writing a book. We can also have a self-conscious work, especially if we refer to a work of art as the intentional product of structures of consciousness, in Edmund Husserl's sense as opposed to the psychological sense of the term. *Reflexivity*, on the other hand, at least as I and some others use the term, need not be a product of consciousness. In the case of literature, it can simply be a reflex of its medium: language. While language often seems to reach out to refer to a world beyond itself, its existence as a system of signs separate from the empirical world causes it to reflect upon itself as language. Since some degree of reflexivity is inevitable in any work of fiction, it should be obvious that reflexivity alone is not the sign of a sophisticated work.

In my study of the book's many returns, I will treat both self-consciousness and reflexivity. When I write about the author's odyssey through the act of writing, I am writing about self-consciousness. When I write about the book's language turning on itself, I am writing about reflexivity. The importance of this distinction should become clear when I describe the book's "tale of the telling." What I will argue is that one reason the reader can make so many happy returns to the pages of *Ulysses* is the author's self-conscious awareness of the reflexive nature of language.

Of course, such self-consciousness about language's reflexivity is not confined to Joyce. I do not claim that Joyce is the only or even the first writer to have it. I do claim, however, that his works, *Ulysses* included, are some of the most effective users of this awareness. In fact, I would even claim that Joyce's works are largely responsible for today's critics' ability in retrospect to see the reflexive nature of all works of literature,[3] since a line of influence can be drawn from Joyce to one of the leading proponents of the reflexivity of language, Jacques Derrida, who once claimed that his work is but a footnote to *Finnegans Wake*. A similar line of influence has already been drawn to those writers of fiction whom critics love to lump together under the label postmodern.

3. For an example of this argument, see Paul de Man, "Criticism and Crisis," in his *Blindness and Insight* (New York: Oxford University Press, 1971), 17. For de Man, the essence of literature is its reflexive announcement of itself as a sign. "The self-reflecting mirror-effect by means of which a work of fiction asserts, by its very exis-

A comparison between Joyce and Vladimir Nabokov, one of those postmodern writers influenced by him, should help clarify one quality of Joyce's writing that distinguishes him from most writers, even some sharing his self-conscious awareness about language. Both Nabokov and Joyce have great respect for the power of language. Here is Alfred Appel on Nabokov: "To Nabokov, the unconnected impressions and associations that impinge on the mind are irrational until they are consciously ordered and to order them in art is to fulfill virtually a moral obligation, for without rational language man has 'grown a very / land-fish, languageless, / a monster,' as Thersites says of Ajax in Shakespeare's *Troilus and Cressida*." Nonetheless, Nabokov faults Joyce for foregrounding words as such: "We think not in words but in shadows of words. . . . James Joyce's mistake in those otherwise marvelous mental soliloquies of his consists in that he gives too much verbal body to words."[4] It is exactly what Nabokov faults—foregrounding the materiality of words—that makes Joyce so interesting to me. By foregrounding words as words, Joyce makes it possible for us to see the workings of his language. So enabled, we can see the reflexive nature of all language.

If labeling Joyce a writer self-conscious about the reflexivity of language, one who continually makes us aware of words as words, helps account for some of the differences we experience in reading *Ulysses* as opposed to other texts, it also seems to catch me in a serious critical bind. A writer self-conscious about language seems to be an author in control of his language. Advocates of literary reflexivity, however, usually assert the opposite: rather than consciousness having priority over language, language has priority over consciousness; hence an au-

---

tence, its separation from empirical reality, its divergence as a sign, from a meaning that depends for its existence on the constitutive activity of this sign, characterize the work of literature in its essence. It is always against the explicit assertion of the writer that readers degrade the fiction by confusing it with a reality from which it has forever taken leave."

4. *The Annotated Lolita*, by Vladimir Nabokov, edited, with preface, introduction, and notes, by Alfred Appel, Jr. (New York: McGraw-Hill, 1970), 375.

thor is not "in control" as we usually think of it. It seems that a critic cannot have it both ways. He must take a stand on this issue.

But both positions risk distorting the relationship between consciousness and language, and both risk ending in solipsism. If language has priority over consciousness, man becomes locked in a prison house of language, and the only alternative to despair is to turn the prison house into a fun house. If consciousness has priority over language, there is a nagging sense of the inadequacy of language to allow man to escape the confines of his individual consciousness. Silence becomes a logical alternative.

More specifically, those arguing for the priority of language over consciousness cannot help but anthropomorphize a text. Thus, they continually write, as I already have, about a text reflecting upon or deconstructing itself. No matter how much free play language might have, it does not play without players to read it. A text is never totally independent of the consciousness that gives it life, even if that consciousness changes from an author to a reader. But if the theoreticians of literary reflexivity fall prey to a modern version of the pathetic fallacy, their strength has been to force a reexamination of what we mean by the terms *author* and *reader*. They have helped us see that in literature language is not merely a tool by which the mind of the author orders the world or expresses an idea or represents subject matter prior to language.

Since I have already granted Joyce a kind of self-conscious control over language that exceeds that of most other authors and since a major part of my thesis is that Joyce, the author, makes self-conscious returns to his text through the act of writing, I should stop for a moment to consider the implications of the argument made by proponents of literary reflexivity. This position has been argued most persuasively by critics from France, critics who have gaily pronounced the death of the author. If the author is dead, I might ask myself how he can return to his text. To do so, I need an obituary on the defunct author: not so much to give definitive answers to these thorny questions as to indicate my own position.

Those raised in the Anglo-American tradition might ask why all the fuss about the recent announcement of the death of the author. Didn't W. K. Wimsatt and Monroe C. Beardsley in "The Intentional Fallacy" kill him off years ago? And hasn't Wayne Booth made the important distinction between the historical author of a text and a text's implied author, warning us not to confuse the "author" we find in a text with a real person outside the text because the implied author is a textual construct? Aren't the French critics just adopting fancy jargon in order to say what their less abstract Anglo-American counterparts said years ago? Not really. The reason is that, by making a split between the empirical and the implied author or the poet and the poet's persona, the Anglo-American tradition leaves the question of the self untouched.

In "The Intentional Fallacy" Wimsatt and Beardsley admit, "A poem does not come into existence by accident. The words of a poem, as Professor Stoll has remarked, come out of a head, not out of a hat. Yet to insist on the designing intellect as a *cause* of a poem is not to grant the design or intention as a standard by which the critic is to judge the worth of the poet's performance."[5] A structuralist, however, would question exactly this privileged status of the self and the designing intellect as cause or source. The experience we have in the acts of writing and reading, in which language constitutes a self (character, persona, implied author, or reader) rather than vice versa, has more than aesthetic consequences for someone like Roland Barthes.

For Barthes, the source of the meaning of a text is not, as critics as different as E. D. Hirsch and Georges Poulet would argue, the author's intention. For Barthes, the author loses his privilege as source because his intention has already been conditioned by a language existing prior to him. The author's language, like the critic's, "is not a gift from heaven; it is one of the range of languages offered by his situation in time and, objectively, it is the latest stage of a certain historical development of knowledge, ideas and intellectual passions; it is a *necessity*." The author can indeed choose "this necessary language, in accordance

---

5. W. K. Wimsatt, Jr., and Monroe C. Beardsley, "The Intentional Fallacy," in W. K. Wimsatt, Jr., *The Verbal Icon* (Lexington: University of Kentucky Press, 1954), 4.

with a certain existential pattern, as the *means of exercising* an intellectual function which is his, and his alone, putting into operation his
'deepest self,' that is, his preferences, pleasures, resistances and obses-
sions,"[6] yet he is not the source of the intellectual function he exer-
cises. We can see this by looking closely at the very notion of authorship. Through the act of writing, the writer submits himself to the role
of author, so that when we speak of an author we speak not of the
empirical self who put pen to paper but of a role defined by texts
prior to the writer's own that have defined the function of author.
Having created the role of author, these texts undercut any claim the
author has to the status of an original source.

My discussion of Joyce's return to the text does not necessarily
contradict this position. While Joyce calls attention to his arrangement
of the language of *Ulysses*, the possibilities he exploits are contained in
an already existing system of language. By adopting so many different
roles as author to employ so many styles and languages to present the
book's naturalistic tale, Joyce shows how a reader's sense of reality is
controlled by "the range of languages offered by his situation in time."
Furthermore, talk as I will about Joyce's return to his text, it can only
occur through language. The Joyce who returns is not the empirical
Joyce but the Joyce defined through the act of writing.

Barthes himself admits that every act of writing implies a subject.

Every utterance implies its own subject, whether this subject be expressed in
an apparently direct fashion, by the use of "I," or indirectly, by being referred
to as "he," or avoided altogether by means of impersonal constructions.
These are purely grammatical decoys, which do no more than vary the way in
which the subject is constituted within the discourse, that is, the way he gives
himself to others, theatrically or as a phantasm; they all refer therefore to
forms of the imaginary. The most specious of these forms is the privative, the
very one normally practised in scientific discourse, from which the scientist
excludes himself because of his concern for objectivity. What is excluded,
however, is always only the "person," psychological, emotional or biographi-
cal, certainly not the subject. It could be said moreover that this subject is

6. Roland Barthes, "Criticism as Language," in *The Critical Moment* (New York:
McGraw-Hill, 1964), 129.

heavy with the spectacular exclusion it has imposed on its person, so that, on the discursive level—one, be it remembered, which cannot be avoided—objectivity is as imaginary as anything else.[7]

This passage helps explain what I mean when I write that "Joyce" returns to his text. The Joyce who returns is that subject implied by every utterance. The initial style of *Ulysses* masquerades as an objective style similar to the scientific discourse Barthes describes, in which the subject seems invisible. But because objectivity is as imaginary as anything else, the subject makes its presence felt with a vengeance in its return after the initial style has been abandoned. This process, by which the subject merges into language and language into the subject, is one that *Ulysses* continually reenacts.

It is my contention that *Ulysses'* self-conscious reflexiveness is neither the despairing result of an inability of consciousness to escape the confines of language nor a humanistic celebration of consciousness' power through language to create order out of chaos. Instead it uses the play of language to escape the solipsistic notions of a consciousness prior to language and of language that can express itself without the existence of a consciousness. Through its reflexiveness *Ulysses* allows us to reexamine the way in which we create linguistic texts (codes) and are in turn created by them. In foregrounding the language of *Ulysses*, Joyce not only exhibits the power he has over words, he also reminds us of the power words have over him and us.

But despite Joyce's fascination with words, an entire strain of *Ulysses* criticism has chosen to ignore, minimize, or complain about the role of language in the book. Critics of this sort might agree with an "inward reflection" of Bloom in "Eumaeus": "there being more languages to start with than were absolutely necessary" (*U* 622.28–29). The most influential of these critics, the critic who has written what Fritz Senn calls "the best book against Joyce," is S. L. Goldberg. Goldberg's work in *The Classical Temper* is important and cannot be ignored. He was one of the first to emphasize Joyce's self-conscious technique of commenting on the creation of *Ulysses* within *Ulysses*.

---

7. Roland Barthes, "Science Versus Literature," *Times Literary Supplement*, 28 September 1967, pp. 897–98.

According to Goldberg, the function of this self-consciousness is to point out the touch of the artist in each one of us. "Joyce's art—in this perhaps like Gide's or Proust's—is in a large part *about* aesthetic theory, about its own creation of meaning in its author's experience of his world so that it may also represent the process and difficulties of every man's creation of meaning in his experience."[8]

I do not want to argue with this aspect of Goldberg's thesis. The way in which we structure coherent works of art—in both writing and reading—has affinities with the way we create a coherent sense of the world we live in. But just because I agree with Goldberg on this point does not mean that I agree with him on others. The mere fact that Goldberg compares Joyce to Proust and especially Gide shows that he does not understand the full implications of Joyce's self-consciousness. For Gide, self-consciousness is a problem of an author's voyeuristic watching of himself; he keeps a notebook about keeping a notebook, etc. Joyce also indulges in such voyeuristic self-consciousness. But he goes beyond it, because of his awareness that reflexivity occurs within language itself; the nature of a book's language shapes it as much as an author's or reader's consciousness. Goldberg could never appreciate this sort of self-consciousness about language because of his own view of language. His understanding of the language of *Ulysses* is the view of Aquinas that Goldberg attributes to Stephen: "Language is the product, or rather expression, of the whole process of apprehension."[9] But, for Joyce, language is neither the product nor the expression of apprehension; it is the very means of apprehension.

Goldberg's view of *Ulysses*' language underlies his major critical assumptions. For Goldberg, an artist who attains the classical temper is freed from false ideals and insecurities so that he can apprehend the world as it is in order to utter its unuttered meaning. Since language is the product or expression of the artist's apprehension, the reader's task is to peel away the husk of language and to uncover the meaning

8. S. L. Goldberg, *The Classical Temper* (London: Chatto & Windus, 1961), 92.
9. *Ibid.*, 70. For an excellent development of the affinities of creation from the standpoint of the reader, see Eckhard Lobsien, *Der Alltag des "Ulysses"* (Stuttgart: J. B. Metzler, 1978).

that the book contains. Such a view of language allows Goldberg to perform a number of critical services for readers puzzled by *Ulysses'* language. In discussing Stephen's Shakespeare theory, a theory that he admits gains its "truth" through Stephen's "concocting" a "biography" from "absurdly" worked-out details, Goldberg does the reader the favor of leaving out Stephen's absurdities and fanciful speculations in order "to sketch out an aesthetic position much less idiosyncratic, but considerably more important, than is always ascribed to Joyce."[10] The result is Goldberg's own tidy four-point paraphrase of Stephen's aesthetics.

What Goldberg, who throughout his book gives great moral force to those who stick to the "now, the here" of experience, fails to realize is that the "now, the here" of reading *Ulysses* is its language. To separate Stephen's theory from the absurdities and concoctions of its particular language is to distort it. Yet it is exactly Goldberg's belief that we can separate Joyce's "statement" from his language that leads him to reject the entire second half of the book, for it is in the second half of *Ulysses* that we are brought face to face with language that refuses to become transparent. Language does not lead us to a direct apprehension of the world but instead reminds us of its existence as language. For Goldberg, the foregrounding of language in the second half of *Ulysses* is like the absurdities and concoctions of Stephen's Shakespeare theory: it is excessive and obscures the book's "real meaning." In other words, the effect of Goldberg's criticism is to use all that he finds "most fundamental; free and vital" in Joyce's work to condemn one of the aspects of *Ulysses* that distinguishes it from traditional nineteenth-century narrative. As A. Walton Litz puts it, "Goldberg has the missionary purpose of saving Joyce from himself and the modern world."[11]

Goldberg's moralistic questioning of the excess of the book's language has found many followers. These critics, like Goldberg, assume

10. Goldberg, *The Classical Temper*, 87.
11. A. Walton Litz, "The Genre of *Ulysses*," in *The Theory of the Novel*, ed. John Halperin (New York: Oxford University Press, 1974), 113. Also see A. M. L. Knuth's response to Goldberg's criticism, "Tyrants More Cruel Than Procrustes Old," in A. M. L. Knuth, *A Wink of the Word* (Amsterdam: Rodopi, 1976), 64–70.

that a reader can know what *Ulysses* is "about" independent of its styles. In touch with this privileged source of information, they are able to criticize the style of certain episodes for not doing what they have decided it is trying to do. Finding the episode's style lacking, they then go on to ask if such stylistic experiments are justified. But how, I ask, do they know what an episode is about, if not through the episode's style?[12]

For an example of this type of argument and how I would answer it, let me cite William Schutte and Erwin Steinberg's criticism of the second half of *Ulysses*.

We may well agree, too, with the critical consensus that Joyce's technical control in individual episodes is brilliant. However, ultimately we must ask whether the formidable displays of narrative technique, impressive as each may be in itself, contribute to an artistically integrated whole. If, as Joyce proposed in his early sketch, man's life is "a fluid succession of presents" whose "individuating rhythm" the artist must "liberate," it is easy enough to make a case for Lestrygonians as reflecting the "individuating rhythm" of Leopold Bloom's present during the lunch hour, or of Nestor and Scylla and Charybdis as reflecting the rhythm of Stephen's present at two separate times on June 16, 1904. However, it is more difficult in these terms to justify the use of the fugue form to suggest the particular rhythm of Bloom's present during the hour he spends in the Ormond Bar. The conscientious reader can hardly avoid certain essential questions. Are the shifting tones of mood, sensation, thought, and feeling which suffuse The Sirens best presented through the complex, formal pattern which the fugue imposes? Do the introductory fragments justify themselves? Or, to move to another section, how can one justify the "show" passages in Cyclops? Are the verbal excesses there really necessary to suggest the presence of Daniel-Bloom in the lion's den? Or again, granting that the catechistic method of Ithaca does reflect the aridity and hopelessness of the present being shared by Stephen and Bloom, is it not perhaps carried well beyond the point where it serves a legitimate function?[13]

---

12. See David Lodge's intelligent discussion of the role of language in fiction, in his *Language of Fiction* (New York: Columbia University Press, 1966).
13. William M. Schutte and Erwin R. Steinberg, "The Fictional Technique of *Ulysses*," in Thomas Staley and Bernard Benstock (eds.), *Approaches to "Ulysses"* (Pittsburgh: University of Pittsburgh Press, 1970), 175–76.

Schutte and Steinberg, like most conscientious readers, admit Joyce's skill. What they object to is (1) the failure of the styles of the individual episodes to fit into "an artistically integrated whole" and (2) the excesses of individual styles to portray the book's naturalistic tale. The New Critical bias of the first objection is obvious. It is my contention that Joyce's narrative strategies do fit together and complement one another, although, if we are to see how, we will have to question and revise our preconceived notions of what makes "an artistically integrated whole," by recognizing the fictional nature of such coherence. As for the second objection, my response to their question about "Sirens" should serve to stake out my position. No, I suppose that Joyce's technique in "Sirens" is not the best way to present "the shifting tones of mood, sensation, thought, and feeling," but it is the best way to present these moods *along with everything else that the chapter does.* In taking this stand, I am not a reader who Schutte and Steinberg claim "is prepared blindly to accept the author as a genius who can do no wrong." I have asked many of the same questions that they have. What I found, however, is that we have a lot of hard work to do to understand the multiple effects of Joyce's language before we are so ready to condemn it for not doing what we decide it should be doing. In other words, it is my contention that a truly conscientious reader of *Ulysses* must be willing to reexamine his fictional preconceptions about what fiction should do, rather than to fit *Ulysses* into those preconceptions.

It is on the crucial status of *Ulysses'* language, and whether we should evaluate it only in terms of its referential function, that I take issue with three important recent studies of *Ulysses*: Marilyn French's *The Book as World,* C. H. Peake's *James Joyce: The Citizen and the Artist,* and James Maddox's *Joyce's "Ulysses" and the Assault upon Character.* But before disagreeing with them, I want to list some of their important contributions to post-Goldberg *Ulysses* criticism. Where Goldberg, for instance, demands resolution of opposites, these three propose that Joyce's fictional world is founded upon the coexistence of opposites. French and Maddox extend this claim to declare that *Ulysses* is founded upon the void of incertitude. As Maddox says, *Ulys-*

ses is "a collocation of details pointing toward an unnamable center."[14] This insight leads French and Maddox to emphasize what has often been stated, but perhaps not emphatically enough: in reading *Ulysses* we become increasingly aware that we know the world through its signatures. But as important as these insights are, Peake, Maddox, and French continue, along with Goldberg, to posit a subject matter and then judge the book according to this subject matter. In other words, they take for granted the very point that *Ulysses* makes us question. To demonstrate how, let me turn first to Peake and Maddox and then to French's metaphor of the book as world.

With their less rigid demands for resolution, Peake and Maddox are less harsh on the second half of *Ulysses* than is Goldberg. Peake, for instance, does not demand a synthesis between artist and citizen, only an interaction. They both do an admirable job of justifying the styles of the later chapters in light of their theses. Both are especially good in intelligently defending "Eumaeus" from its detractors. But, finally, if I were Schutte or Steinberg or Goldberg, I would still not be convinced that the stylistic experimentations of the second half were justified. The fault, however, does not necessarily lie in Joyce's writing; it may be in the assumptions Peake and Maddox adopt to justify the chapters. Those assumptions become clear in their dismissals of "Oxen of the Sun." Both reject the chapter for failing to do what it should be doing, although what it should be doing for Peake differs from what it should be doing for Maddox. In other words, both continue to assume, as Goldberg does, that a novel has a referential subject prior to its language. For Peake, this subject is "a profound, extensive and coherent vision of life"; for Maddox, it is the "essential" selves of the characters that, although unnamable, are established in the first half of the book. Peake maintains that the objections to Joyce's extravagant styles "can be answered only if it can [be] shown that the complexities of the work, so far from being a disproportionate burden, are made to strengthen and sustain the action, and enrich and

---

14. James H. Maddox, *Joyce's "Ulysses" and the Assault upon Character* (New Brunswick: Rutgers University Press, 1978), 15, 168.

extend its significance." Maddox, on the other hand, defends *Ulysses'*
extravagant language because Joyce, by using "style as obfuscation,"
demonstrates that language cannot capture the mystery at the core of
human existence. Peake justifies the styles of the second half as part of
a coherent world view; Maddox, as an unsuccessful attack on the coherence of character.[15] One defends the styles for sustaining the action, the other for screening us from it.

My claim is that the language of the second half can do both. We
can best understand how Joyce can accomplish these and other seemingly contradictory effects, by recognizing that the book invites us to
read it two ways. On the one hand, *Ulysses'* exacting realism invites
us, as French's title reminds us, to read the book as world. On the
other, its reflexiveness warns us to read the book as book. To read the
book as world means to apply the insights we learn from the book to
life, and vice versa. We realize, as Maddox and French emphasize, that,
like a book, the world and the self can be known only through a system of signs, that we continually read the world according to linguistic
codes. Furthermore, by reading the book as world, we start to apply
our knowledge of the world to the book. Thus, characters come alive,
and we treat them as real people who act like people we know. We
apply our behavioral and ethical standards to them. For instance, introduced to Bloom in the earlier chapters, we indeed start to feel that
his essential nature is screened from us by the stylistic mannerisms of
the later chapters, that the later styles distort the Bloom we know.
French posits a narrator for the second half of the book whose anti-
humanistic stance, as embodied in the styles of the different episodes,
mocks Bloom's warm "humanity." Thus, by a strategy of indirection
Joyce affirms the *caritas* that French feels underlies his vision. Or as
Robert Story, influenced by French and Goldberg, argues, the late
styles, by calling attention to themselves as styles, allow Bloom to assume "the status of an elusive and ungraspable man, not a 'character.'"
"What is happening [in "Eumaeus" and "Cyclops"] is that Bloom's

15. C. H. Peake, *James Joyce: The Citizen and the Artist* (Stanford: Stanford University
Press, 1977), viii, 119–22; Maddox, *Joyce's "Ulysses" and the Assault upon Character*,
15, 168.

speech insists upon its literary origin and function; consequently, his reality as a 'character' is undermined, while his freedom as an autonomous human being, who transcends all reportorial and presentational modes, is implied."[16]

Yet the moment we speak of the language of the book as screening us from what is really going on or as limiting the freedom of characters, we blind ourselves to reading the book in a second way: not as world but as book. Through the self-conscious acknowledgment of his book as book, Joyce continually warns us against reading the book as life. Whenever we try to make a connection between the book and life, we are reminded that the connection we make is based on a fiction. In other words, the moment we make the move from book to life, the book reminds us of its counterfeit nature. The only way in which the book can escape its counterfeit masquerade is to ask the reader to look at it as what it really is—a book. Viewed in this way, the essential nature of Bloom remains such a mystery not because, existing prior to language, it resists definition by language but because there is no essential Bloom prior to words. As a character in a book, Bloom is a verbal construct, and it is only in a very limited context that we can say that language is inadequate to capture Bloom or anything else in *Ulysses*. Whereas Wisdom Hely advertises his existence by having men march through the streets of Dublin masquerading as letters, Bloom exists as a result of words marching across the pages of *Ulysses*. In "Circe," Joyce lets the Watch remind us of Bloom's linguistic existence by declining his name as a part of speech. "Bloom. Of Bloom. For Bloom. Bloom." Immediately thereafter, the First Watch remarks, "Caught in the act" (*U* 453.20, 23), which may apply to Joyce as well as to Bloom. In "Eumaeus," Joyce goes so far as to let Bloom unwittingly remark on his ontological status, "though in reality I'm not" (*U* 643.4). Moreover, while Maddox and French argue that the language of the second half screens us from Bloom, the reader's sense of Bloom depends as much on the language of the second half of the book as on

16. Marilyn French, *The Book as World* (Cambridge: Harvard University Press, 1976); Robert Story, "The Argument of *Ulysses*, Reconsidered," *Modern Language Quarterly*, XL (June, 1979), 195, 193.

that of the first, for, as Peake shows, in addition to creating the illusion that it screens us from Bloom, the language of the second half also reveals much about him. To see how much, we need only compare an early draft of one of the later chapters to the final text to watch Bloom change as the language changes.

No doubt, some readers will object that to read the book as book will ruin all that is most valuable about *Ulysses* by neglecting the human story. But let me make clear that I am not ruling out the possibility of reading the book as world; perhaps we cannot help but do so. What I am saying is that, as we read this book whose "whole galaxy of events, all [go] to make up a miniature cameo of the world we live in" (*U* 646.41–42), the book's language calls attention to itself in such a way as to remind us that our connection between book and world depends on a rhetorical figure, a simile. We are reminded of the *as*. One way in which we are reminded of the *as* is by the fact that this world of words has been shaped by James Joyce, who has in turn been shaped by the words he uses. Our encounter with the "Joyce" constituted by the language of *Ulysses* has its own rewards and offers its own reflections. "Still, to cultivate the acquaintance of someone of no uncommon calibre who could provide food for reflection would amply repay any small . . . Intellectual stimulation as such was, he felt, from time to time a firstrate tonic for the mind" (*U* 646.35–38).

What reading the book as book might cause us to reflect upon is our own unexamined assumptions about the world we live in. If we remember that the book is only a book, we become aware that we turn that book into a world by bringing our sense of the world to bear upon it. As a result, the book might provoke us into questioning whether what we believe is given "in" the world might not be the result of our own construction of it. To take one example, even those who sense an essential Bloom as they read the book admit that his essence is not contained within the book, since the book's language cannot represent it. Therefore, they might be called upon to question whether their discovery of an essential Bloom does not depend upon their own belief in the existence of autonomous human beings, a belief that the book's language forces us at least to reconsider. Moreover, I would argue that a willingness to read the book as book should eventually enhance our reading of the book as world because it introduces the important Joycean theme that our understanding of the world is conditioned by books, works of art, and language.

The way in which reading the book as book can enhance our reading of the book as world is demonstrated by Hugh Kenner's recent work. In *Joyce's Voices*, Kenner tells us that the only "real" action of the book is its own styles. "Still we may suppose that there is after all a 'truth' recoverable from beneath all these surfaces, a truth the writer could put straightforwardly if he wanted to. There is not." But this does not mean that Kenner no longer appreciates the book's human story. Quite the contrary. His appreciation of the human story seems to have sharpened over the last twenty years of rereading the words of *Ulysses*. In *Dublin's Joyce* we hear Bloom's mind referred to as "a compost of objects" and of his "complete narcotic immersion in his environment"; in *Joyce's Voices* we hear of Bloom's "unflagging alertness" and "the detailed tug of his plight on our human sympathies."[17] As Kenner argues, if we can rid ourselves of the belief that the story exists prior to the book's language, we will be better able to give the book's language proper attention and learn how its rhetoric is connected with Joyce's naturalistic intentions. How this is done is the topic of Kenner's most recent book: *Ulysses* by Hugh Kenner.

Despite Kenner's work and a growing critical awareness that a novel's language is not simply referential, almost all the recent studies of *Ulysses* continue to try to uncover the book's hidden meaning. But trying to uncover *Ulysses'* meaning independent of its language is to indulge in the myth that our relation to the world is not conditioned by language. Therefore, even though I know that much work will continue to be done on *Ulysses* in terms of character, plot, and theme, I have decided to emphasize what I call the book's tale of the telling rather than the book's naturalistic tale. It is my contention that one reason that *Ulysses* is so important in the history of the novel is that it reminds us once again that in prose fiction the tale of the telling is as important as the telling of the tale.

17. Hugh Kenner, *Joyce's Voices* (Berkeley: University of California Press, 1978), 91, 62; Hugh Kenner, *Dublin's Joyce* (Boston: Beacon, 1962), 174, 170.

What I call the tale of the telling has affinities with what the Russian formalists call "baring the device," acknowledging the devices by which a work of art is constructed. This is part of what Boris Tomashevsky calls a work's artistic motivation, which is differentiated from realistic motivation, or those aspects of a text trying to establish the reality of the naturalistic tale. While the Russian formalists took care to describe different motifs in a work, some artistically motivated and some realistically, one of the special qualities of *Ulysses'* language seems to be its ability to be simultaneously artistically and realistically motivated.[18] In *Ulysses* the same words that advance the naturalistic story also advance the tale of the telling. For instance, statements such as Buck's, "The most beautiful book that has come out of our country in my time. One thinks of Homer" (*U* 216.27–28), fit perfectly into the naturalistic context while reminding us of the book's Homeric legacy, something no character is aware of.

The book's Homeric correspondences are merely one of the most obvious parts of the tale of the telling. Briefly, the naturalistic tale exists as a function of the plane of action between reader and character, while the tale of the telling exists as a function of the plane of action between reader and author.[19] In the tale of the telling the reader is continually instructed as to how to read the book. Joyce, that textbook example of the author who shows rather than tells, in his own way offers commentary to the reader as obtrusively as a Fielding or a Thackeray. But in order to hear the author's comments, the reader

18. *Russian Formalist Criticism: Four Essays*, trans. Lee T. Lemon and Marion J. Reis (Lincoln: University of Nebraska Press, 1965). I do not want to simplify the Russian formalists' understanding of artistic and realistic motivation. For them no one motif necessarily contributes to artistic or realistic motivation. The motivation of a motif depends on its context. The point is, however, that in a particular work we can usually decide which motifs contribute to realistic motivation and which ones to artistic motivation.

19. Marilyn French, *The Book as World*, 67, discusses the triangular relationship between the text, narrator, and reader. Arnold Goldman, *The Joyce Paradox* (Evanston: Northwestern University Press, 1968), 78, adopts the term *the drama of the alternatives*. My tale of the telling is related to but different from these two formulations.

cannot play a passive role. He has to be able to switch his mental set from naturalistic tale to tale of the telling and back again.

Ulysses' language is like the famous gestalt figure of the rabbit-duck.

 Rabbit or Duck?

We can see the drawing as either rabbit or duck, depending on how we look at it. The figure has no one "meaning"; its meaning changes according to the context in which we place it. Yet that context can be changed merely by switching perspective within our minds. Our minds are flexible enough to see it one way and then to switch perspective and see it the other, although, as E. H. Gombrich warns, we cannot see both rabbit and duck at the same time.[20]

In a similar manner, the language of *Ulysses* can change meaning not because we change anything on the page but because we shift the perspective from which we read it. The meaning of a word or phrase depends upon its context and the mental expectations of the reader. Part of the magic of *Ulysses'* language is its ability to create multiple contexts that in turn lead the reader to expect and thus create even more contexts. The result is that a trivial word or phrase can become a treasure chest of potential meanings. The simple listing of English vowels becomes a sentence in *Ulysses*: "A.E.I.O.U." (*U* 190.3) By exploiting the inherent flexibility of language, Joyce turns *Ulysses* into an extended pun wherein the meaning of words changes with the expectations we bring to them.

20. See E. H. Gombrich, *Art and Illusion* (London: Phaidon Press, 1972), 4. The rabbit-duck continues to be a source of critical debate. For a summary, see James Kincaid, "Coherent Readers, Incoherent Texts," *Critical Inquiry*, III (Summer, 1977), 781–802.

One effect of my concentration on the tale of the telling should be to alert the reader to aspects of the book's language he might never have noticed because of his expectations of what language in a novel should do. Trained by countless novels (and critics) to read all the book's language as referring to the naturalistic tale, the reader might close himself to the rich potential of *Ulysses'* language. But to be so closed off is to miss some of the most important play of a book whose language emphasizes its protean nature.

The tale of the telling, as far as I have described it, is self-consciously created by Joyce. Yet as we have seen, one of its most important functions is to draw attention to the way in which *Ulysses* creates a world out of words. It is through the tale of the telling that we are invited to pay attention to the book's language, including its reflexivity. Thus, the tale of the telling ultimately comes to include even the play of language not consciously "intended" by Joyce.

In following the tale of the telling as it moves from self-consciousness to reflexivity, from Joyce's conscious intention to the play of language, in the first three chapters I treat Joyce's self-consciousness about general problems of representation and how it leads to his authorial return through the act of writing. These chapters describe the larger structure of the return story pattern. But then, in an important turn, I link the book's circularity to the nature of its language. Thus, the next three chapters look more closely at the book's language. That is not to say that I attempt a stylistic study. Instead, I am concerned with demonstrating its polytropic nature and, most important, trying to describe the reader's role as he encounters this language.

Further, there are three sections (two chapters each), foregrounding, respectively, the turns and returns of author, text, and reader. The sections are not rigorously exclusive, however, as these convenient labels—author, text, and reader—continually merge. For instance, in the last two sections I start by returning to the role of the author in order to trace a movement to the reader through the text.

The first chapter of the first section places *Ulysses* within a general theory of the novel as a self-conscious genre; the second emphasizes how Stephen's Shakespeare theory is a justification for Joyce's self-conscious return to his text and his use of the return story pattern.

The middle section, which marks the turn in my argument, is the short-est. Its first chapter examines the implications of structuring *Ulysses* by the universal return story pattern. Its second chapter draws some conclusions about the turning nature of the book's language, especially its proper names. Finally, the last section consists of discussions of the process of reading and the interpretive models the text offers to guide us on our journey through the book's pages.

My final port of call before starting the book proper will be a word about my emphasis on the role of the reader. In emphasizing the role of the reader, I might be accused of transferring to the reader the role of meaning-maker traditionally assigned to the author, a strategy advocated by some so-called reader-response critics. As Jonathan Cul-ler remarks, "Literary study experienced what Barthes called 'the death of the author' but almost simultaneously it discovered the reader, for in an account of the semiotics of literature someone like the reader is needed to serve as center." But Culler's next sentence makes clear that an emphasis on the reader need not turn him into the origin of the meaning of a text. "The reader becomes the name of the place where the various codes can be located: a virtual site." In other words, the role of the reader as much as the role of the author can be seen to be a product of textual conventions. Roland Barthes puts it this way: "The 'I' which approaches the text is itself already a plurality of other texts, of infinite, or, more precisely, lost codes (whose origins are lost). . . . Subjectivity is generally thought of as a plenitude with which I encumber the text, but in fact this faked plentitude is only the wash or wake of all the codes which make up the 'I,' so that finally my sub-jectivity has the generality of stereotypes."[21]

What such semiotically based textual models tell us is what any sophisticated phenomenological model already acknowledges: the ques-tion of meaning is a question of process. The concern is not to locate meaning in either subject or object but to transcend the Cartesian subject-object dualism that contributed to establishing the old model. Sophisticated reader-response criticism can, without conferring priv-

21. Jonathan Culler, "In Pursuit of Signs," *Daedalus*, CVI (Fall, 1977), 108; Roland Barthes, *S/Z* (Paris: Seuil, 1966), 16.

ileged status on the reader, point out the reader's active as well as passive role in constituting texts.

One of the most interesting accounts of the reader's role in Joyce's texts is Colin MacCabe's *James Joyce and the Revolution of the Word*. MacCabe claims that "reading for us is passive consumption; with Joyce it becomes an active metamorphosis, a constant displacement in language." Although engaged in an active process, the reader still does not have dominance over the book's language.

Joyce's texts, however, refuse the subject any dominant position from which language can be tallied with experience. *Ulysses* and *Finnegans Wake* are concerned not with representing experience through language but with experiencing language through a destruction of representation. Instead of constructing a meaning Joyce's texts concern themselves with the position of the subject in language. If the literary critic is interested in meaning, Joyce's texts are concerned with the various positions from which meaning becomes possible. In order to grasp the activities of Joyce's texts it becomes necessary to understand the construction of the possible subject and the position of the subject and what is always buried in that construction. Joyce's texts disrupt the normal position assigned to a reader in a text and thus alter the reader's relation to his or her discourse. This disruption is not merely a formal matter but also determines Joyce's concerns on the level of content.[22]

I agree with much of what MacCabe has to say. For me, the reader's role is also active, if not dominant. I also examine, if less theoretically, the subject's position in language—including character, author, and reader. I agree that *Ulysses* disrupts the relationship of the reader to the text that convention has established as the "normal" one. My attempt to show the shared concerns of the tale of the telling and the naturalistic tale tallies with MacCabe's discovery of similar concerns on levels of form and content. Nonetheless, I have a major disagreement with MacCabe, which is reflected in the discourses we adopt to try to describe the experience of reading *Ulysses'* language.

MacCabe aligns himself with someone like Culler, who advocates a special role for the critic. For MacCabe, in place of interpretation,

22. Colin MacCabe, *James Joyce and the Revolution of the Word* (London: Macmillan, 1978), 2, 4.

"we might begin the study of the positions offered to the subject within language and of how literature confirms and subverts those possibilities." I agree with MacCabe about the importance of such an emphasis. I disagree, however, that such studies take the place of interpretation, since (and this is a lesson I would claim Joycean texts teach us) even an attempt to study the positions offered the subject within language is a form of interpretation. As MacCabe's use of an annotation, in Don Gifford and Robert J. Seidman's *Notes for Joyce*, of a passage in "Scylla and Charybdis" shows, MacCabe relies on the annotation to make a passage clear.[23] But Gifford and Seidman's annotation is not the only way to interpret the passage. MacCabe bases his description of the position of the subject on a prior act of interpretation.

Further, I can point to the radical difference between MacCabe's interpretation of what Stephen's Shakespeare theory implies for the reader and the interpretation I will offer in the last chapter. Unlike MacCabe, I admit that I continually interpret, even going so far as to enter "the happy hunting-ground of all minds that have lost their balance" (*U* 248.34–35) to try to answer the question, Who was M'Intosh? Not to indulge in such hunts is to miss much of the mock-serious play of *Ulysses*. More important, not to risk interpretation is to avoid the dialogue between text and reader that allows the subject to discover the positions offered to him within language.

I think that one of MacCabe's problems lies in his use of the word *meaning*. The long passage of his that I quote betrays his lapse into the objectivist-positivist notion of meaning, which he tries to go beyond. We can agree with MacCabe that Joyce's texts do not "construct" a meaning and still hold out for the need to interpret. So long as we think of *meaning* as a noun, we will tend to treat it positivistically, as if it were a thing that we could touch. But if we remember that *meaning* is a gerund, we will be reminded that it is not a thing but a process.[24]

23. Jonathan Culler, "Beyond Interpretation: The Prospects of Contemporary Criticism," *Comparative Literature*, XXVIII (Summer, 1976), 244; MacCabe, *James Joyce and the Revolution of the Word*, 2, 118.
24. See W. Wolfgang Holdheim, "The Lessons of Phenomenology," *Diacritics*, IX (June, 1979), 31.

Meaning occurs through the process of reading, and all reading requires interpretation. As MacCabe himself admits, there is no innocent reading prior to interpretive models. The danger of interpretation comes when we reify a process and turn *meaning* into a noun. The very mode of critical discourse may make that reification inevitable, but we can at least acknowledge our failures without trying to make the reading of criticism as challenging as the reading of *Ulysses*.

My introduction should make clear that I do not attempt a progressive "reading" of *Ulysses*. I avoid this chapter-by-chapter approach not only because I agree with MacCabe that at this stage of *Ulysses* criticism we do not need one more critic to make available to the public his personal reading of the entire book but also because it is the nature of my topic to assume that my reader, having worked his way through the book a number of times in a linear fashion, is now ready to read from back to front to middle, following the book's language as it leads us on many happy turns and returns. Of the self-consciously reflexive works in our literature, *Ulysses* is one of our most flexible. Demanding a reader with reflexes to match its own, it is forever capable of responding to changing situations. *Polytropos*, indeed.

Part I

A Lord of Language

Chapter One

A Chance Word Will Call Them Forth

My odyssey through *Ulysses* starts with an ingenious hero who traveled far and wide but returned to Dublin from a self-imposed exile only through the imaginative act of writing. Further, not only had this self-styled hero exiled himself from historical Dublin, he also seemed to have exiled himself as author from his imaginative re-creation of it. To quote again that passage in *A Portrait of the Artist as a Young Man*: "The artist, like the God of creation, remains within or behind or beyond or above his handiwork, invisible, refined out of existence, indifferent, paring his fingernails" (*P* 215). The subject of my first two chapters is Joyce's self-conscious return to his handiwork called *Ulysses* through styles and devices that become most noticeable in the second half of the book. But a return implies a previous departure. Before we can understand Joyce's return to his text we need to understand why he wanted to give the impression of an artist refined out of existence. As Stephen tells us in "Scylla and Charybdis," "There can be no reconciliation . . . if there has not been a sundering" (*U* 195.7–8).

Stephen's proclamation of artistic invisibility in *A Portrait* places Joyce's early fiction within the tradition of Flaubert. Just as Stephen lifts his idea of the artist from a remark in one of Flaubert's letters, so Joyce models his early fiction after that of Flaubert. Flaubert opens *Madame Bovary* in the first person, but within a few pages third-person narrative takes over and distantly and ironically describes the action of the novel. Similarly, Joyce opens *Dubliners* with three stories in the first person, only to yield to the aloof third-person narrative of the next twelve stories.

Not only the narrative technique but the subject matter of Joyce's early fiction have similarities with Flaubert's. Both Flaubert and the early Joyce write the fiction of solipsism. Imprisoned in the paralysis of their limited points of view, the characters in these fictions place themselves at the center of the universe and create a fictional view of the world. Standing in a godlike position outside his creation, the artist can expose the limitations and failings of a character's solipsism. But the artist himself does not necessarily move beyond the prison of solipsism that he portrays. He too creates a fiction that masquerades as the real world.

What Flaubert learned, however, was the ability to hide the act of artistry by which he constructed his fictional world. He did so by developing the style of objectivity. According to Jonathan Culler, an objective style is not necessarily one that withholds opinions or judgments so much as one that tries "to prevent the text from being recuperated as the speech of a characterizable narrator, to prevent it, that is to say, from being read as the vision of someone who becomes an object that the reader can judge. The language of the text will organize the world, select details, offer judgments, shift its perspectives, adopt momentarily various modes of discourse and types of speech that can be identified, but it does not create for us a personality whom we feel we know."[1]

For Hugh Kenner, the style of objectivity is the style adopted by literary counterfeiters. Counterfeiting a world that pretends to write itself, the Flaubertian artist, like all good counterfeiters, tries not to draw attention to his act of forgery. Thus, he works with scrupulous care to make his world of words correspond to the world his words profess to represent. Joyce's early development as a writer can be seen as a mastering of the style of objectivity with the resulting ability to produce counterfeits. It is this craft of forgery to which Stephen,

1. Jonathan Culler, *Flaubert: The Uses of Uncertainty* (Ithaca: Cornell University Press, 1974), 83.

unwittingly, calls our attention at the end of *A Portrait* when he goes forth to forge in the smithy of his soul the uncreated conscience of his race (*P* 253).

By the time of *Ulysses*, Joyce counterfeits Dublin, 16 June 1904, so accurately that he has caused unprecedented critical problems. In order to understand more fully the naturalistic tale of *Ulysses*, Clive Hart and Leo Knuth decided to produce *A Topographical Guide*, which traces all the characters' wanderings through the Dublin streets. Hart has even used a stopwatch while walking the paths the characters take in "Wandering Rocks" to see which actions occur simultaneously.[2] Furthermore, critics and readers continue to confuse the "real" Dublin with the counterfeit one Joyce forged in *Ulysses*, a confusion encouraged by Joyce, who scatters the names of real people within the pages of his book just as cubist painters learned to include real scraps of newspaper in their collages. As a result, poor Dr. Richard Best had to protest to a BBC interviewer, "I am not a character in a fiction. I am a living being" (*JJ* 374).

In this light, it is interesting to imagine Joyce reading the book *Literary Forgeries* by J. A. Farrer, published in 1907. The fourteenth chapter is appropriately entitled "The Immortal Hoax of Ireland" and refers not to the country but to William Henry Ireland, who in 1796 forged a Shakespeare play—just as Joyce has Stephen forge a Shakespeare biography. The introduction to Farrer's book is even more appropriate for Joyce. It is by none other than Andrew Lang, who earlier had translated the *Odyssey*. We can imagine Joyce smiling if he read: "Indeed, if we believe Greek literary tradition, literary forgery was common as soon as the art of writing was used for literary purposes. . . . We might begin with the Homeric poems, of which by far the greater part, if we accept a prevalent theory, is a sort of literary forgery, though done, as a rule without intent to deceive." Originally of oral composition, the Homeric poems were preserved in print by people other than their author. Therefore, the *Odyssey* itself helped launch the tradition of counterfeiting. The historical novel, Lang asserts (and *Ulysses* proves), belongs to this tradition. Noting the diffi-

2. Clive Hart, "Wandering Rocks," in Clive Hart and David Hayman (eds.), *James Joyce's "Ulysses"* (Berkeley: University of California Press, 1974), 215–16.

culty of distinguishing between forgeries and the "genuine forgeries" (*U* 634.25) of art, Lang describes readers' reactions to his own attempt to write a historical novel. "It was a blunder, if not a crime, for a learned mediaevalist could not make out whether he had a modern novel or a 15th century document in his hands, while the novel-reading public exclaimed, 'Oh, this is a horrid real history!' Let this be a warning to historical novelists."[3] If Joyce read this passage, he did not heed its warning. Instead he chose to perpetuate the crime.

But if Joyce confused people through his style of objectivity, he confused even more by abandoning his initial style of objective presentation for the noticeable styles of the later chapters. Having constructed such a convincing counterfeit, why does Joyce seem intent on exposing his artistry by scattering evidence of his forgery throughout *Ulysses*? The change in technique can, I believe, be understood in light of the "crime" involved in the novelist's attempt to counterfeit a world.

We can better understand Joyce's return to his handiwork by looking at Joyce in a tradition of the novel as "a self-conscious genre," to use Robert Alter's phrase. According to Alter, many novels challenge the "ontological status" of fiction by creating a "quixotic tension between what is fictional and what is real."[4] The novel lends itself to self-consciousness because of its demand to represent a world. What its self-consciousness indicates is that a novel does not so much represent a world as offer an interpretation of a world. The work of two critics writing at the same time as Joyce acts as a useful way of looking at the novel in this way. The year 1914 marks not only Joyce's first work on *Ulysses* but also the completion of José Ortega y Gasset's *Meditations on Quixote* and the first draft of Georg Lukács' *The Theory of the Novel*.

Lukács links the birth of the novel to the Renaissance's invention of man's interiority. This is because, for Lukács, "the novel tells of the adventure of interiority; the content of the novel is the story of the soul that goes to find itself, that seeks adventures in order to be

---

3. Andrew Lang's introduction, in J. A. Farrer, *Literary Forgeries* (London: Longmans, Green, 1907), xiii–xv.

4. Robert Alter, *Partial Magic* (Berkeley: University of California Press, 1975), 224.

proved and tested by them, and, by proving itself, to find its own essence." But, in searching for his essence, man comes face to face with a vast material world of seemingly senseless connections. This world of sheer brutal "materiality" is a world beyond man's control. "The totality of life, forever, resists any attempt to find a transcendental center within it, and refuses any of its constituent cells the right to dominate it." Yet this is exactly what the hero of the novel and the novelist himself try to do. Therefore, the novel, like no other form, is an expression of this transcendental homelessness. As the novelist sits at his writing desk, trying to re-create the world out of his head, "what is given form here is not the totality of life but the artist's relationship with the totality, his approving or condemnatory attitude towards it; here, the artist enters the arena of artistic creation as the empirical subject in all its greatness but also with all its creaturely limitations."[5] The inbuilt "bad conscience" of the novelist grows out of the fact that the world he creates poses as the real world, while in reality it is merely his interpretation of the world.

Thus, for Lukács, the development of the novel seems intricately connected with Descartes' *Cogito ergo sum*. By placing all in doubt except the absolute certainty of the self, Descartes' philosophy leads to the assumption that things exist, for a man at least, only because he thinks them. Defining man as subject turns everything else, including God and all creation, into object. Man, once a created being among other created beings, now becomes, like the novelist controlling the world of his creation, the measure of all things. J. Hillis Miller summarizes this development of the novel. "The drama has all moved within the minds of the characters, and the world as it is in itself is by implication unattainable or of no significance. Love, honor, God himself exist but only because someone believes in them."[6]

Ortega y Gasset also places the birth of the novel in the Renaissance. But while Lukács' theory of the novel takes as its point of departure the subjective nature of fiction located in man's interior, Ortega starts by emphasizing the novel's objective nature located in a

5. Georg Lukács, *The Theory of the Novel*, trans. Anna Bostock (Cambridge: Massachusetts Institute of Technology Press, 1971), 89, 53.
6. J. Hillis Miller, *The Disappearance of God* (New York: Schocken Books, 1965), 12.

world of facts. It is no surprise that, despite starting from these op-posite poles, Lukács' and Ortega's theories both lead to an affirmation of the novel's inherent self-consciousness. This is because the Renais-sance man's discovery of inner subjectivity also leads him to discover an outer world of random, objective facts. The mating of the two seems to have led to the birth of the novel as a genre.

Ortega calls the sheer brutal "materiality" contained in the novel the realm of "realistic poetry." Epics, romances, and novels are all nar-ratives. But where epics narrate larger-than-life actions, and romances narrate adventure and chivalry, novels narrate the commonplace ac-tions of everyday life that are neither incredible nor adventurous.

The novel, then, which on one hand contains a hero on an adven-turous Icarian flight searching for his pure essence, on the other surrounds the hero's subjective quest with adventureless, everyday circumstances. The circumstances into which the hero is thrust, an ir-reducible, depersonalized, material world of random, contingent facts without beginning or end, acts as a force of gravity pulling characters who believe in the myth of adventure back to earth. The novelistic hero, like everyman, is forced to confront a world that absorbs his project and materializes it, solidifies it, and turns it into a thing; life becomes a perpetual aspiration and a perpetual frustration. Thus the subject of all novels can be said to be the education of illusions. The novelistic hero tries to fit the world into the mind-forged forms of his imagination, but the world continually resists any attempt to be en-shrouded in the garb of myth, philosophy, religion, or artistic form.

Nonetheless, Ortega argues, reality alone is not a fit subject for poetry. It cannot exist alone. Therefore, even though the novel con-tinually demythologizes, it carries within it the world of the imagina-tion it takes such care to subvert. It is for this reason that the novel is born when Cervantes places Don Quixote at the intersection of the world of reality and the world of myth. Don Quixote, the reader of novels of fantasy, believes in adventure and chivalry. The realistic novel in which he is a character portrays the tension between his fictional beliefs and the everyday world. "The fact is that what is related in the books of chivalry has reality in the imagination of Don Quixote, who, in turn, enjoys an unquestionable existence. So that, although the realistic novel was born in opposition to the so-called novel of fantasy, it carries adventure enclosed within its body."[7] In other words, the de-mythologizing force of the novel that absorbs man's project to find an essence is opposed by what Ortega terms "the concrete destiny of man": the reabsorption of circumstances. Just as circumstance materi-alizes man's imaginary projects, his imagination continually incorpo-rates his circumstance into the project known as man.

Need I add that the novelist has the same project as his hero? He, too, is confronted with a random world without end that he tries to shape into a form with both beginning and end. He has the paradoxical task of both putting the mirror up to a contingent world without form and creating a form to contain that world. No novelist can discount the power of man's imagination, since his novel exists partly as a result of that power. Yet, at the same time, he realizes that the form created by his imagination has the same existence as that of his novel: a fic-tional one.

As Edgar Dryden succinctly summarizes, in his book on Melville, "Only the most naive novelist can be so self-forgetful as to offer his work as though it had made itself, and then we do not see it as he does but rather view it as an expression of his own individuality. The self-conscious novelist is painfully aware of his fiction as fiction. He rec-ognizes the subversive implications of his demiurgical acts and un-derstands that his own presumptuous world is ultimately unified by personal and largely arbitrary choices, with the result that the novel becomes self-reflexive and develops a bad conscience." Iris Murdoch is even more succinct. She says that all novelists carry with them a "meta-physical regret."[8]

The novel, then, results from Western man's locating truth within the human intellect, as opposed to Indian and Chinese sages who insist that man cannot attain truth so long as he remains locked up in his intellect. In fact, if a novelist rigorously pursues the assumptions of the

7. José Ortega y Gasset, *Meditations on Quixote*, trans. Evelyn Rugg and Diego Maria (New York: W. W. Norton, 1961), 143–45, 137.
8. Edgar Dryden, *Melville's Thematics of Form* (Baltimore: Johns Hopkins University Press, 1968), 6; Iris Murdoch, "The Novelist as Metaphysician," *Listener*, XVI (March, 1950), 473.

cogito upon which the novel is based, he ends by calling the absolute certainty of the self into doubt. For example, Samuel Beckett's Cartesian first-person narrator in *The Unnamable* denies his own thoughts and existence.

As Dryden reminds us, almost all major novelists have inevitably sensed the egocentricity of their point of view; thus the novel's inbuilt "bad conscience." In other words, Flaubert's invisible artist-god does not exist. He always betrays his existence in his created world. Wayne Booth's *The Rhetoric of Fiction* exhaustively documents example after example to point out that, even in works that have no direct authorial intrusion à la Trollope or Fielding, the artist still seems to make his presence felt, by the manner in which he orders and arranges his material. In *Madame Bovary*, for instance, some consciousness beyond Emma's juxtaposes the events of the agricultural fair with Rodolphe's attempted seduction in order to produce the hoped-for effect of irony. Someone has chosen the *mot juste* or the appropriate symbol to structure a scene. By the very control of his material the author seems to reveal his presence as the creator of the text from which he has tried to disappear. As Hugh Kenner remarks, "Nothing is as dependent as Objectivity on language and the rituals of language, Objectivity which had promised to evade rhetoric and make facts effect their own declaration."[9]

It is this betrayal of objectivity within objectivity that Booth fails to understand about novelists like Flaubert or Joyce. To quote Kenner again, they have learned "the lesson of generations of counterfeiters who restored the personal to a blank universe by seeming to suppress the person."[10] Flaubert posits the existence of a narrator who knows from the start how the action will unfold, by starting *Madame Bovary* in the first person. Soon this authorial consciousness disappears, but, having already been incorporated into the contours of the fiction, it undermines the possibility of a purely dramatic narration. Joyce is careful to have Stephen include the preposition *within* to describe one of the artist-god's possible relations to his text, although critics too

9. Hugh Kenner, *Joyce's Voices* (Berkeley: University of California Press, 1978), 14.
10. Hugh Kenner, *The Counterfeiters* (Bloomington: Indiana University Press, 1968), 99.

often overlook it. To be sure, we are only beginning to see all the implications of the irony of having Stephen Dedalus proclaim this doctrine of artistic impersonality in a work that has traditionally been read as autobiographical.

Implicitly acknowledging and feeling guilty about the novelist's point of view, however, does not eliminate the crime. For some novelists, the answer seems to lie in fully confessing the crime while perpetuating it. Even this confession does not solve the problem. In *Under the Net*, Iris Murdoch tells us, "Yes that's the grand style of lying. Put down your best half truth and call it a lie, but let it stand all the same. It will survive when your qualifications have been forgotten, even by yourself."[11] In *Ulysses*, however, Joyce never lets us forget his qualifications. Through the noticeable styles and attention-getting devices of the second half Joyce continually reminds us that his work has not made itself. The notion of the artist hiding behind a distant mask of objectivity has been rejected.

Hugh Kenner marks this as the move from *fin de siècle* solipsism to modernism:

Release from the prison of late 19th-century pictorial analogies came when the teller was let back into the tale.

Flaubert had wanted the artist, lonely as God, to be somewhere outside of his work, which is impossible: impossible because words are said by somebody; because—at the furthest remove from the intimacies of breath—a bicycle saddle and handlebars, even when no sculpturing hand molests their shapes, denote by their power to combine into a bull's head a possibility some human eye has seen (Picasso saw it, 1943). Art does not "happen." The vision that made it is part of it. The eye of vision sees systems of connectedness; this may not *be* that, but it has the same structure. A bull's form, some drawn lines, are so similar that we "recognize" a picture of a bull, but part of the picture is the mind that conceived it.

For Kenner, *Ulysses* ushers in the modernist era in literature: "Joyce made the penultimate breakthrough, as Pound and Eliot (and later the Williams of *Paterson*) quickly perceived. On 19 December 1917 Ezra Pound read the first 17 pages of *Ulysses* in typescript. In the next three

---

11. Iris Murdoch, *Under the Net* (New York: Random House, 1954), 72.

years he and Eliot gradually came to know half the book as *The Little Review* and *The Egoist* serialized it."[12]

In fact, Joyce himself traces an odyssey of a disappearing and returning artist. If we chart the development of Joyce's work, keeping Stephen's categories in *A Portrait* of lyric, epic, and dramatic in mind, we find that at first Joyce follows Stephen's prescription and increases his narrative distance from the text. So, from the lyric stage of *Chamber Music* he progresses to the epic stage of *Stephen Hero* and finally the distant dramatic stage of *Dubliners*, *A Portrait*, and *Exiles*. Then, however, he reverses his movement. In *Ulysses* the distance between himself and his work of art decreases, placing *Ulysses*, a retelling of the *Odyssey*, where it belongs, in the epic stage. Finally *Finnegans Wake* ends where Joyce began, in the lyric. This remark needs elaboration.

It goes without saying that the "lyrical" mode in *Finnegans Wake* is different from the lyrical mode in *Chamber Music*, for it has developed out of the epic and dramatic modes of the previous works. One way of understanding this development is to look at Joyce's use of the first- and third-person points of view. While *Dubliners* starts with three stories in the first person and then moves to the third, all Joyce's later works start in the third and end in the first. In *Finnegans Wake*, however, the movement becomes circular. Since the last word of the book leads us back to the first word of the book, we change point of view from first to third in mid-sentence. What we are reminded is that, while the third person is generally thought a more objective point of view than the first, for Joyce the third is never quite that objective and the first never quite that subjective.

In other words, an important effect of Joyce's manipulation of point of view and his movement from apparent narrative invisibility to apparent narrative presence is to go beyond the subject-object dualism that has plagued the novel since its birth coincided with the development of the Cartesian cogito. In going beyond the limitations of subject-object thinking, the techniques of *Ulysses* coincide with a different sense of reality starting to reassert itself in the early years of

12. Hugh Kenner, *The Pound Era* (Berkeley: University of California Press, 1971), 32–33, 381.

the twentieth century. Buckminster Fuller summarizes this new general law. "Heisenberg said that observation alters the phenomenon observed. T. S. Eliot said that studying history alters history. Ezra Pound said that thinking in general alters what is thought about." Or as Ortega argues in his important essay, "The Doctrine of the Point of View," "The persistent error that has hitherto been made is the supposition that reality possesses in itself, independently of the point of view from which it is observed, a physiognomy of its own. . . . Perspective is one of the component parts of reality. Far from being a disturbance of its fabric, it is the organizing element. A reality which remained the same from whatever point of view it was observed would be a ridiculous concept."[13] Reality resides neither in the perceived nor in the perceiver but in an interaction between the two. Furthermore, while reality is dependent upon perspective, it cannot be dominated by a single perspective.

Ulysses' tale of the telling accounts for perspective as a component part of reality by admitting a "stupendous innovation—the existence of the author." This appeal for authors to acknowledge their existence appears in a 1934 article, "Recent Irish Poetry." It is written wittily enough under a pseudonym. The author turns out to be none other than Joyce's onetime friend in Paris—Samuel Beckett. Because of Joyce's strong influence upon Beckett at this time, Beckett's argument bears looking into. Beckett distinguishes between truly modern Irish poets and those he calls antiquarians by how aware they are of "the new thing that has happened, or the old thing that has happened again, namely the breakdown of the object, whether current, historical, mythical or spook." This breakdown has led to a "rupture of the lines of communication." "The artist who is aware of this may state the space that intervenes between him and the world of objects; he may state it as a no-man's land, Hellespont or vacuum, according as he happens to be feeling resentful, nostalgic or merely depressed. A picture by Mr. Jack Yeats, Mr. Eliot's 'Waste Land,' are notable statements of this kind. Or he may celebrate the cold comforts of apperception.

13. *Ibid.*, 162; José Ortega y Gasset, "The Doctrine of the Point of View," in his *The Modern Theme*, trans. James Cleugh (New York: Harper & Brothers, 1961), 90.

He may even record his findings, if he is a man of great personal courage."[14] An artist of great courage, Joyce is not afraid to record the findings of apperception.

As a result, *Ulysses* avoids succumbing to what Ortega calls the primitive point of view in art.

The "primitive" painter depicts the world from his point of view, that is, in obedience to ideas, valuations and sentiments which are peculiar to him; but he believes that he paints it as it is. For the same reason he forgets to introduce his own personality into his work; he offers us the work as if it had made itself, without the intervention of any particular agent; it is fixed at a definite position in space and at a definite moment in time. We naturally see in his picture the reflection of his own individuality and thus do not see it as he did, since he took no account of himself as a person and believed himself to be the anonymous pupil of an eye spontaneously opening upon the universe. This habit of not taking any account of the self is the magic source of ingenuousness.[15]

In no way does Joyce forget to introduce his personality into his work: in *Ulysses* he adopts a method similar to that of Jan van Eyck in *Giovanni Arnolfini and His Bride* or Velázquez in *The Maids of Honor* or Botticelli in *Adoration of the Magi*, all of whom, like Stephen's painter of old Italy, set their faces in a corner of their canvas (*U* 209.32–34). The presence of Joyce's fingerprints within his handiwork validates the action of *Ulysses* much in the manner that van Eyck, appearing in the mirror, serves as a witness validating the marriage he paints. As we read in "Nausicaa": "Wants to stamp his trademark on everything" (*U* 378.7–8).

Ulysses, then, confronts the reader with the paradox of an artist who at first seems totally removed from his handiwork, but who on closer inspection returns to leave traces of his presence within his handiwork. This paradox splits *Ulysses* critics into two camps. One group emphasizes Joyce's objectivity; the other, his subjectivity. Taken alone, neither is a fair assessment, but it is easy to see how the contro-

---

14. Samuel Beckett [Andrew Belis], "Recent Irish Poetry," *Bookman*, LXXXVI (August, 1934), 235–36.
15. Ortega, "The Doctrine of the Point of View," 93.

versy arises. As both Lukács and Ortega argue, the novel develops out of a tension between portraying man's subjective interior and an objective world of random facts. No world of fiction embodies these tensions more than Joyce's. *Ulysses* exhausts the genre of the novel because it simultaneously stretches the two poles of the novel as far as they can go. The more Joyce exposes man's interiority, the more he surrounds it with a world of irreducible material facts. We have both Stephen's solipsistic walk on Sandymount Strand and a detailed account of the Dublin water system.

Ulysses carries extreme subjectivity within its pages in the figure of Stephen. By having Stephen play the role of Hamlet, Joyce exposes the cords connecting *Ulysses* to the *omphalos* of the novel by exploring the strandentwining cables (*U* 38.2) of the history of man's discovery of his own interiority. Hamlet, who could have lived in the nutshell of a closed world of subjectivity if it were not for a conscience producing bad dreams, is a perfect example of the Cartesian novelist and his accompanying bad conscience. When a watered-down version of Hamlet appears as an Irishman in 1904, he is transformed into Joyce's figure for the subjective artist par excellence. At the end of his school days in *A Portrait*, Stephen goes forth to welcome life and "encounter for the millionth time the reality of experience" (*P* 252–53). As an artist he hopes to use the smithy of his soul creatively to hammer that experience into a unified whole. But man, as Hamlet knows, can only rough-hew his ends; he cannot shape them. Stephen, therefore, embodies Lukács' definition of the novel as the story of the soul that goes forth to find itself by seeking adventures, to be proved and tested by them, but the soul runs the risk of forging the world to fit its own image.

In carrying subjectivity within its pages in the figure of Stephen, *Ulysses* is similar to *Don Quixote*, which carries romance in its pages in the figure of Don Quixote. And just as *Don Quixote* moves narrative into a new era, so does *Ulysses*. Through Stephen, Joyce stretches that aspect of the novel expressing man's transcendental homelessness to its end point, causing it to turn back on itself in parody, including Stephen's own self-parody.

A major force behind this parody is the factuality of the world into

which Stephen is thrust. Stephen, who tries to deny his bodily existence, cannot cope with materiality. Yet, the quotidian world is always
there, acting as a force of gravity to ground his imaginative flights. As
Wallace Stevens says, "The imagination loses vitality when it ceases to
adhere to what is real." Fully aware of the effect of his technique,
Joyce told Arthur Power, "In realism you are down to facts on which
the world is based: that sudden reality which smashes romanticism
into a pulp. What makes most people's lives unhappy is some disappointed romanticism, some unrealizable or misconceived ideal. . . .
Nature is quite unromantic. It is we who put romance into her, which
is a false attitude, an egotism, absurd like all egotism. In *Ulysses* I tried
to keep close to facts."[16]

But the world of material facts itself is extended so far that it too
falls prey to parody, as, for example, in the exhaustive lists of "Ithaca."
As Joyce added more and more detailed facts to the text he did not
approach an objective presentation of reality but lists ordered according to the preexisting schema of the catechism. Far from random,
these lists of facts hint at patterns of meaning. Even the inventory of
the contents of Bloom's drawer becomes significant. Thus, as Joyce so
vividly sees, a novel both places a mirror up to a contingent world of
nature and forges that world into a structure promising meaning.

Furthermore, that meaning can only come alive through another
act of interpretation, an act of reading. If the author's perspective is a
component part of the world he creates in his novel, so is the reader's
perspective a component part of the world of words he interprets.
When the artist abandons his position outside his handiwork for a self-
conscious return within it, he changes his relationship with his reader.
The effect on his reader of Joyce's tale of the telling can be seen within
the Flaubertian tradition and in terms of a breakdown of a theory of
representation that posits a split between subject and object.

Jonathan Culler defines the reader's role in reading Flaubert,
by reference to the reader's role in reading pre-Flaubertian novels.

16. Wallace Stevens, *The Necessary Angel* (New York: Knopf, 1951), 116; quoted in
Clive Hart and Leo Knuth, *A Topographical Guide to James Joyce's "Ulysses,"* Vol. I, *Text*
(Colchester: A Wake Newslitter Press, 1975), 7.

While not all pre-Flaubertian novels would fit Culler's schema, his for-
mulation is helpful. According to Culler, the fundamental convention
of the pre-Flaubertian novel is "a pact of community between author
and reader, signalled in various ways by the narrative language." This
community is based on the assumption that reader and author share a
world of experience to which the words of the text refer. To read
them is to identify this world—in Culler's words, "to read is to recognize." But our reading process does not stop with recognition. Reading, for Culler, involves a cyclical movement on the reader's part between text and world. "The first step takes him from text to that of
which it speaks. He must identify in the world the referents towards
which the text gestures. Then, having given meaning to the signs of its
histoire, he can move back and read its *discours* as a commentary on
what he has recognized." Culler identifies the second moment of contact, "when the novel becomes an instrument for creating meaning,"
as the one in which critics usually locate a novel's value.[17]

Some fiction, however, disrupts the reader's normal cyclical pattern by breaking the pact of community between author and reader,
thus "demoralizing" (Flaubert's term) the reader. One way in which
demoralization can take place is by blocking the process of recognition, by making the reader read a text as an autonomous verbal object
governed by its own laws with no reference to the world that we expect it to represent. *Finnegans Wake* is a prime example of this strategy. Flaubert, however, chooses to demoralize the reader in the second step, the move from the recognized world back to the text. In
Flaubert, recognition must take place, but rather than allow the reader
to use the text to unify the world and make it intelligible, Flaubert con-
tests our attempts to unify the world according to the models of interpretation established by the text.

Ulysses occupies such a strategic position in the study of novelistic
reading conventions because its conventions lie between those of *Finnegans Wake* and those of *Madame Bovary*. In its first chapters *Ulysses*,
like *Madame Bovary*, posits a recognized world. But by the second half
of the book, not only is our movement from the world of experience

17. Culler, *Flaubert*, 83, 84, 85.

to the text blocked, as in *Madame Bovary*, but the first step, the process of recognition, is also blocked. Nonetheless, having been introduced to a recognizable world in the first half, the reader continues to posit it in the second half, despite the fact that some late chapters of *Ulysses* call attention to their existence as autonomous verbal objects as much as does *Finnegans Wake*.

It is exactly through self-consciously "baring the device" that Joyce alters the Flaubertian reading conventions. As I have argued, *Ulysses*' tale of the telling reestablishes the pact between author and reader—but with an important difference. No longer do author and reader share a world and a faith in language's referential function; instead they share the experience of trying to create meaning through language. Thus, *Ulysses* is not as much about the represented world as about our attempt to represent it, or the tale of the telling is as important as the telling of the tale.

One important result of the pact of community between author and reader found in *Ulysses* is that the author loses his privileged status over the reader. In Flaubert, the reader becomes like Emma, who is continually frustrated in her attempts to make the world conform to a text. Meanwhile, the author sits in a detached position, seemingly superior to the reader's and characters' blindness. In *Ulysses*, however, Joyce starts with the pose of the detached narrator only to abandon it later in the book. He, as much as the reader and the characters, is frustrated in his attempt to move beyond his own interpretive schemas. So at the very moment that the reader of *Ulysses* finds his attempt to move from the world back to the text frustrated, he also confronts an author laughingly sharing and acknowledging his frustration. As I will argue in the last section, the reader's and the writer's roles begin to merge. To use Culler's terms, if the reader of Flaubert finds the *discours* inadequate to make meaning out of the *histoire*, the reader of *Ulysses* finds that the *discours* establishes a *histoire* of *discours*.

One could, as many recently have, deconstruct this entire historical construction—from pre-Flaubertian reading conventions, to Flaubertian ones, to Joycean ones—by pointing out that *Don Quixote*, the first novel, is also the first antinovel. It raises many of the problems of fictional representation, recuperation, and demoralization that Culler talks about as originating with Flaubert. These concerns seem to be generic not historical. As Culler asserts, the genre is "an interpretation of experience, an attempt to make sense of the world . . . a study of the process of reading."[18] It inevitably includes a fictional account of how people read the world according to the interpretive strategies of fiction. Representation seems always to be involved with problems of interpretation and, one could argue, vice versa.

In trying to establish a history of a genre, we too often succumb to the pointed thinking that designates certain names—Flaubert, Joyce—as points of departure, forgetting that the way in which they contest our conventional reading habits has been contested before. The history so established is not really one of chronology and direct influence. Joyce is not only working with Flaubertian reading conventions, he is also reacting against the same sort of "pre-Flaubertian" reading conventions that Flaubert reacted against. The notion of representation was as dominant in Joyce's time as in Flaubert's, and, as the assumptions of many Joycean critics indicate, it is still there today for novelists to react against.[19]

An important danger of establishing a history of a genre is that critics misread texts in order to fit them into a preconceived history. This danger is clearly illustrated in Robert Alter's "history" of the self-conscious strain in the novel. Alter groups Joyce with other modern writers to distinguish them from Laurence Sterne. "In Sterne consciousness constantly transforms reality, but there are no brooding metaphysical or metahistorical doubts about the stuff of reality. In Joyce, Faulkner, Proust, and Virginia Woolf, the stuff of reality, whether considered as personal history, cultural heritage, or metaphysical substratum, threatens to crumble into emptiness, and so the play of consciousness becomes a sustained act of desperate courage—a 'violin in the void,' in Nabokov's memorable phrase—creating form and substance where perhaps there would be nothing."[20]

This account distorts both Sterne and Joyce. I would not want to

---

18. Culler, *Flaubert*, 18.
19. Colin MacCabe, *James Joyce and the Revolution of the Word* (London: Macmillan, 1978), 27, sets Joyce's work against George Eliot's and claims that Joyce's foregrounding of the materiality of language ensures Joyce's fissure with classical realism.
20. Alter, *Partial Magic*, 142.

discount a bit of metaphysical brooding on Joyce's part, but then I would not want to do the same for Sterne either. To me, Joyce's comic spirit seems more closely aligned to Sterne's on this point than to, say, Virginia Woolf's.

Alter works so hard to turn Joyce into a despairing modern that he isolates a passage of Bloom's interior monologue ending, "no one is anything" (*U* 164.37), as proof. Alter claims that this passage is a perfect example of "the Wandering Rocks section of *Ulysses*, the one section in which Joyce offers an explicit panorama of life in the Dublin streets." Thus, his point is made. In the chapter that many critics cite as the one in which Joyce gives his firmest sense of the "now, the here" of Dublin, he has his main character question the stuff of human reality. The problem is, however, that Bloom's passage actually occurs in "Lestrygonians." So when Alter goes on to generalize from this passage that "what is imparted to the reader instead of a solid-seeming reality (as in Dickens and Balzac) is a phantasmagoric dissolution of external reality in the quick solvent of the mind,"[21] he forgets that Bloom's impressions are naturalistically motivated. He is hungry. As the passage continues: "This is the very worst hour of the day. Vitality. Dull, gloomy: hate this hour. Feel as if I had been eaten and spewed" (*U* 164.38–39). Alter's sense of what a modernist writer is forces him to emphasize Joyce's subjectivity at the expense of Joyce's objectivity.

Nonetheless, to admit the dangers of establishing a history of the genre that Alter's misreading reveals is not to overlook the possibility that it would be equally dangerous to pretend that a history does not exist. The experience of reading *Ulysses* is different from reading *Don Quixote*, and part of that difference is a result of the historical circumstances in which they were written. And not only have historical circumstances changed, so too the dominant models by which we interpret those circumstances have changed—a change brought about in part, no doubt, by novels that have challenged outdated models. In *Ulysses* we can watch the challenging of one of the traditional metaphors for artistic representation: the book as mirror. There are far more mirrors than Wilde's cracked looking glass of a servant decorating the walls of Joyce's house of fiction.

21. *Ibid.*, 141.

To be sure, some of Joyce's uses of the mirror metaphor are quite conventional. If Joyce does not think of art as a simple mirror held up to nature, in much of his early fiction he works within the expressionist tradition that knows that art reflects the self as much as nature. By looking at a mirror, a character can expose pretentious fantasies about himself. For instance, the boy narrator of "Araby" concludes: "Gazing up into the darkness I saw myself as a creature driven and derided by vanity: and my eyes burned with anguish and anger" (*Dubliners* 35). Seeing his reflection in the mirrorlike darkness, the boy finally reaches a moment of self-awareness. No longer able to seek escape in romantic notions of love and heroism, he is forced to confront himself. At the end of "The Dead," Gabriel experiences a similar moment of revelation: "He saw himself as a ludicrous figure, acting as a pennyboy for his aunts, a nervous well-meaning sentimentalist, orating to vulgarians and idealizing his own clownish lusts, the pitiable fatuous fellow he had caught a glimpse of in the mirror" (*Dubliners* 220). Then, in *A Portrait*, after Stephen's first attempt to order an experience by composing a poem, "he went into his mother's bedroom and gazed at his face for a long time in the mirror of her dressingtable" (*P* 71). The attempted act of placing his life in art forces Stephen to reflect on himself. This use of the mirror continues into the early chapters of *Ulysses*. Bloom remembers Molly returning home after the first night that Blazes Boylan catches her eye. Concerned with her fading attractiveness, she looks at herself in a mirror. "The mirror was in shadow. She rubbed her handglass briskly on her woollen vest against her full wagging bub. Peering into it. Lines in her eyes. It wouldn't pan out somehow" (*U* 69.34–37). Molly rubs her glass as does the queen in *Snow White*, hoping that her magic mirror will proclaim her the fairest of them all. But the mirror cannot lie. She is forced to confront the fact that she is aging and her looks show it.

The danger of the idea that art is a mirror held up to the self is that it can lead to narcissism and solipsism. If art continually reflects back an image of the artist, the artist cannot see beyond himself and becomes locked in a prison of mirrors. Joyce includes this use of the mirror in his works as well. The narcissistic nature of both Polly Mooney in "The Boarding House" and Gerty MacDowell in *Ulysses* is revealed when they practice expressions in a mirror. But what is most interesting about Joyce's use of the mirror in *Ulysses* is the way in which it avoids the lure of narcissism by going beyond the conventions of the expressionist theory.[22]

Ulysses' mirrors do more than passively reflect life or a self. Within the representational tradition the problem with the mirror metaphor is that the mirror remains stationary as it records what it sees, be it world or artist. While world and artist might change and develop, the point of view from which they are represented remains fixed. But a revolution in fictional technique occurs when, as a budding novelist raised on the dogmas of romanticism and naturalism, Joyce realizes that his perspective is part of the world that he is expected to imitate. Originally conceiving of his art as a mirror held up to himself or his world, Joyce realizes that he is the forger of the mirror that he uses. Therefore, the mirror influences and is influenced by what it reflects. Fictional representation of the world changes with this awareness.

It is easy to speculate on how Joyce came to this awareness. Friends knew that Joyce used his immediate world of Dublin, including them, as his subject matter. That awareness might well have caused them to alter the subject matter. Richard Ellmann chronicles Gogarty's disgust at being "reported" as a character in a work of art, a disgust that influenced his actions toward Joyce (*JJ* 154). And no doubt, the knowledge that he would use himself in his fiction had to alter Joyce's character. Finally, even the seven years during which *Ulysses* was written affected Joyce's thought about his book. By serially publishing the first chapters before the final ones had been completed,

---

22. Joyce of course is not the only novelist to alter the traditional metaphor of the book as a mirror. Stendhal, for example, in the Preface to *Armance* (1827), writes of the novel as a mirror, "qu'on promène au long d'un chemin." Like Joyce's mirror-within-a-mirror metaphor, this metaphor accounts for the movement of point of view.

In his essay "On Impressionism," Ford Madox Ford acknowledges that an attempt to see the world transparently reflects back an image, if not of the author, at least of someone behind him. "Impressionism exists to render those queer effects of real life that are like so many views seen through bright glass—through glass so bright that whilst you perceive through it a landscape or a backyard, you are aware that, on its surface, it reflects a face of a person behind you." Frank MacShane (ed.), *The Critical Writings of Ford Madox Ford* (Lincoln: University of Nebraska Press, 1964), 41.

Joyce wrote the later chapters in light of the criticism of the earlier ones in reviews and letters from such people as Ezra Pound.

The awareness that the mirror changes what it reflects and is in turn changed by it leads to the technique of a mirror within a mirror. As we are told about Bloom in "Oxen of the Sun": "He is young Leopold, as in a retrospective arrangement, a mirror within a mirror (hey, presto!), he beholdeth himself" (U 413.4–6). Leopold can behold himself in a mirror within a mirror because this technique acknowledges point of view as a component part of reality; that is to say, it, as much as that which it reflects, is caught in a temporal world and always moves with time.

As early as his 1904 essay "A Portrait of the Artist," Joyce had been concerned with the ability to capture the past that is a "fluid succession of presents, the development of an entity of which our actual present is a phase only." This means that someone intent on a portrait must find a fluid technique in order to avoid the error of freezing the past. The danger of a fluid notion of personality, however, is the tendency to consider the self new each moment. Stephen toys with this notion in "Scylla and Charybdis" only to reject it when he thinks,

Wait. Five months. Molecules all change. I am other I now. Other I got pound.

Buzz. Buzz.

But I, entelechy, form of forms, am I by memory because under everchanging forms. (U 189.36–40)

The self is not new each moment because the self is not a substance with a static form but a form within time. Therefore, a true portrait "is not an identificative paper, but rather the curve of an emotion."[23] The mirror-within-a-mirror technique acknowledges this temporal component of the world by showing that a point of view is itself part of the temporal world. It gives a moving rather than a stationary point of view.

Once more a digression to Joyce's earlier fiction will help explain

23. Robert Scholes and Richard Kain (eds.), *The Workshop of Daedalus: James Joyce and the Materials for "A Portrait of the Artist as a Young Man"* (Evanston: Northwestern University Press, 1965), 60.

how he arrives at this cubistlike technique capable of capturing a fluid portrait. In *A Portrait* and, perhaps by accident, in the first three stories of *Dubliners*, Joyce moves toward the mirror-within-a-mirror technique that will acknowledge the fluidity of the past without succumbing to total relativity. Developing this technique involves Joyce's effort to place the past in a retrospective arrangement. In this sense the last twelve stories of *Dubliners* are different in kind from the first three. While the three stories of childhood look back and try to understand a past experience, the last twelve hypothesize possible James Joyces of the future. The persona of Little Chandler is what Joyce might have become if an early marriage had forced him to take a job as a clerk. Gabriel Conroy is the possible Joyce if, having become a language teacher, he had married a girl from Galway and remained in Dublin. *Ulysses* incorporates the theme of what one might have become through both Stephen's and Bloom's musings. Stephen intriguingly wonders: "Had Pyrrhus not fallen by a beldam's hand in Argos or Julius Caesar not been knifed to death? They are not to be thought away. Time has branded them and fettered they are lodged in the room of the infinite possibilities they have ousted. But can those have been possible seeing that they never were? Or was that only possible which came to pass? Weave, weaver of the wind" (*U* 25.14–20). Bloom echoes this by simply wondering, "If we were all suddenly somebody else" (*U* 110.24). Then in "Ithaca" he wonders what he might have been and what he might become.

But the childhood stories of *Dubliners* try to recollect the past without questioning the infinite possibilities that it has dislodged. Their first-person narrator reconstructs the past from a perspective that is distanced in time from the events reconstructed. Thus, the story simultaneously includes the boy's experience and the older self's perspective on the experience.

In *A Portrait* the same double perspective exists. The first-person narrator has yielded to a third-person narrator, increasing the illusion of objectivity, but the effort to place the past in a retrospective arrangement remains. The growth of Stephen's early consciousness is reflected by the consciousness that he becomes. Some critics explain this by saying that we watch the fluid growth of the mind that later comes to write the book. But more important is the simultaneity of perspectives. We see both Stephen's perspective as he reacts to a situation and, implicitly, the narrator's perspective on Stephen's reaction. So when Stephen finally discovers his vocation at the end of Chapter 4, the reader senses both Stephen's excitement and the irony of the narrator who undercuts Stephen's Icarian soaring by juxtaposing a scene of boys diving into the water crying, "O, cripes, I'm drownded!" (P 169)

Later Stephen begins to develop the narrator's capacity for irony, as when he catches himself incorrectly remembering Thomas Nash's line "brightness falls from the air": "He had not even remembered rightly Nashe's line. All the images it had awakened were false. His mind bred vermin. His thoughts were lice born of sweat of sloth" (P 234). But even this scene of self-correction is undercut if the reader has read the note in a 1904 edition of Nash's poetry—available to Joyce—that explains that the line should probably read "brightness falls from the hair."[24] Thus, the symbolist connotations making the line beautiful to Stephen also ring false. Not only does he quote the line incorrectly, he quotes a line whose value is a forgery.

A Portrait, however, despite its sophisticated use of double perspective, remains a mirror, not a mirror within a mirror. The aloof narrator places Stephen's growth in a retrospective arrangement, but he remains outside the book's action. With no present perspective actively participating in the book, the interaction of perspectives is more static than dynamic. Unlike Stephen's growing consciousness, the narrator's perspective is fixed and does not change in time. Pointing to the two dates on the final page of A Portrait—1904 and 1914—Hugh Kenner argues that in actuality the narrator's perspective is not fixed.[25] While placing twenty-two years in retrospective arrangement, the narrator has moved ten years in time. Thus, a dynamic interaction of

24. "It is to be hoped that Nash meant 'ayre,' but I cannot help strongly suspecting that the true reading is 'hayre,' which gives a more obvious, but far inferior sense." Robert B. McKerrow (ed.), Thomas Nash—Works (5 vols.; London: Bullen, 1904–1910), IV, 440.
25. Hugh Kenner, "Joyce's Portrait—A Reconsideration," University of Windsor Review, I (Spring, 1965), 1–15.

perspectives operates. But in *A Portrait* the narrator does not draw attention to his shifting perspective. With the narrator standing outside his handiwork in the immovable position of God, the book seems to be written from a fixed point in time.

In *Ulysses*, however, where the narrator returns to participate in his creation, his perspective continually shifts as it interacts with the past that it arranges. The point of view from which the story is told becomes a part of the story, acting and reacting with its other elements. This interaction of perspectives establishes the "self-reflecting mirror-effect" of *Ulysses* by which, according to Paul de Man, a work of fiction asserts its separation from empirical reality.[26] A mirror within a mirror, *Ulysses* takes on aspects of a closed system generating its own force fields of interacting parts with an existence now independent of the demands of mimesis. Each of the book's styles and points of view participates in this interaction, continually modifying one another. Thus, no one point of view is privileged. The "truth" of the book lies in the energized space produced by the never-ending, dynamic interaction of these perspectives, perspectives awaiting a reader to activate them.

As a result, chapter after chapter of the book can be considered a mirror reflecting the action of the rest of the book, influencing it and being influenced by it. "Wandering Rocks," for instance, centrally located as the first chapter of the second half, provides a mirrorlike glimpse of Dublin between the hours of three and four. As Leo Knuth points out, the physical center of the chapter is defined by Merchants' Arch, where Bloom searches for a book for Molly. This is approximately the spot where Father Conmee's path if extended would almost intersect with the viceregal cavalcade. The section in which this occurs, the tenth, is also the central section of the chapter's nineteen. Organized around this center, the chapter is structured with a bilateral symmetry. For instance, the state (in the form of the viceregal cavalcade) in the nineteenth section gives a mirror reflection of the Church, seen in Father Conmee's walk in the first; Corny Kelleher surveying a coffin

---

26. Paul de Man, "Criticism and Crisis," in his *Blindness and Insight* (New York: Oxford University Press, 1971), 17.

in the second balances the son of recently buried Paddy Dignam in the eighteenth; and the lame sailor of the third reflects the blind stripling of the seventeenth.[27] Mirrorlike reflections occur throughout the chapter. "At the Howth road stop Father Conmee alighted, was saluted by the conductor and saluted in his turn" (U 223.13–14). Or, "on the steps of the City hall Councillor Nannetti, descending, hailed Alderman Cowley and Councillor Abraham Lyon ascending" (U 246.15–17). The lackey of Dillon's auction room, Mr. Kernan, John Fanning, and Dignam's two sons all peer at themselves in mirrors. Phrases from one section are mirrored in other sections thirty-two times. Phrases, actions, and thoughts are mirrored from other chapters. Like Stephen and Bloom, Father Conmee reminds himself of a letter, and like Bloom, he wonders why there isn't a tramline along an important thoroughfare. Even Bloom and Stephen have their mirror images in Bloom the dentist and the blind stripling.

Three other chapters acting as mirrors within mirrors are found toward the end of the book. These three, "Oxen of the Sun," "Circe," and "Ithaca," all place the action of the book in "retrospective arrangement"—a phrase repeated six times throughout the last nine chapters (U 241.4, 277.18–19, 413.4–5, 444.22, 651.39, 724.24). Each of these chapters uses one of three important techniques of Ulysses in an exaggerated form as they bring together most of the major themes and events of the book. "Oxen of the Sun" utilizes the technique of parody as it gathers the medical students and their friends plus Stephen and Bloom for a drunken round of storytelling that simultaneously recapitulates the history of the English literary language, the growth of a fetus, and the action of Ulysses to that point.

Immediately following "Oxen of the Sun," Bloom enters Nighttown by passing two mirrors—one concave and one convex. The mirrors of "Circe" are indeed "mocking mirrors" (U 576.8), a phrase that mocks the use of the phrase in the second chapter (U 28.16). Appropriately, the world of "Circe" generates a bizarre, antirealistic reflection of the book's action by using the exaggerated technique of magi-

27. Leo Knuth, "A Bathymetric Reading of Ulysses, Chapter X," James Joyce Quarterly, IX (Summer, 1972), 405–22.

cal symbolism. Virtually everyone and every object turn up in "Circe," in strange and distorted visions. But, despite its distortion, the mirror of "Circe" imparts new meaning to previously random characters and events by rearranging them in a different way. The mirror of "Ithaca," on the other hand, is controlled by the world of science. Here the technique of scientific naturalism is carried to its extreme in order to try to give an exact reflection of the book's action. In exact prose the chapter details facts and dates about Bloom, Stephen, and their environment, in encyclopedic fashion.

Ironically, however, as Joyce extends these techniques to their limits, each acquires characteristics of its opposite. In "Circe" the anti-realistic distortions are rendered with the utmost precision. The effect is to undercut the power of Bloom's fantasies. For instance, the description of Rudy when he appears to Bloom, "*dressed in an Eton suit with glass shoes and a little bronze helmet*" (U 609.21–22), reveals Bloom's sentimentality at the same time that it evokes our sympathy. It mocks our tendency to give the scene overtones of the Resurrection. The technique of "Ithaca" works in the opposite direction. Originally forcing us to see Bloom and Stephen demythologized, as depersonalized objects in a vast cosmos, "wanderers like the stars at which they gaze" (*Letters*, I 159–60), the technique increasingly moves toward symbolism as the detailed descriptions create a new mythology of meaning for Bloom's and Stephen's actions.[28] Once again, Giordano Bruno's coincidence of contraries is at work.

The perspective of *Ulysses*, of course, is not the isolated reflection of one of these mirrors within a mirror but the total effect of all the interacting reflections. Taken alone, none of the mirrors gives a complete reflection of the book's action. Each illuminates certain aspects of the book better than others. And because we have access to what is illuminated in other chapters, we can label each chapter in itself inadequate in mirroring the book's totality. Taken together, the mirrors have the effect of reminding the reader of the infinite perspectives needed to create the parallax to see the world wholly. In terms of reading the book, the vast number of points of view that comprise the

28. A. Walton Litz, "Ithaca," in Hart and Hayman (eds.), *James Joyce's "Ulysses,"* 385–405, provides the best explanation of this aspect of "Ithaca."

text increases the indeterminacy of the reader's response. Rather than having one sure perspective to rely on, the reader, as soon as he feels comfortable with one perspective, is forced to adopt a new one. Struggling to maintain a consistent reading, the reader himself must fill in the *Leerstellen* created as the text leaps from one perspective to the next. While this demand on the reader increases his participation within the text, it also increases his tension over his inability to be certain of the "correct" reading.[29]

By isolating in pure form the three major techniques of his book in these three chapters, each reflecting the total action, Joyce creates an ecological system of interacting perspectives all necessary to the working of the whole. These points of view are not static. They are in constant metamorphosis, because in the process of reflecting the book's action a chapter adds to that action, thus modifying the perspective of the other two mirrors within a mirror. Thus, although Joyce bounds his book by a wall of mirrors, we can never locate one fixed perspective from which we can evaluate the action.

So we have another paradox. In *Ulysses*, Joyce refuses to indulge in the illusion that a work of art creates itself by including within its pages the perspective from which it was created. But by including his perspective as a component part of his work, he creates a work of art that seems capable of rewriting itself. In other words, Joyce gains a new objectivity, not by abandoning his subjectivity, but by accounting for it. By including his own point of view without giving it privileged status, Joyce combats the bad conscience of the novelist, whose treatment of things other than himself always seems arbitrary. By returning to his text, Joyce, who once aspired to become an artist-god, admits the limitations of his point of view as an artist; and, by returning home, Odysseus and Bloom admit their limitations as men.

The first sentence of *Ulysses* testifies to the increased objectivity Joyce allows himself with this new technique. "Stately, plump Buck Mulligan came from the stairhead, bearing a bowl of lather on which a mirror and a razor lay crossed" (*U* 2.1–3.2). Rather than continuing to

29. See Wolfgang Iser, "Indeterminacy and the Reader's Response in Prose Fiction," in J. Hillis Miller (ed.), *Aspects of Narrative* (New York: Columbia University Press, 1971), 1–45.

focus on his alter ego, Stephen, Joyce begins with a description of Buck Mulligan, not as Stephen sees him, but as an omniscient narrator does. To be sure Stephen is not far away; he physically enters the book within thirteen lines and shortly thereafter we descend into his mind. Even so the narrator of *Ulysses* has gained the confidence objectively to treat a character other than Stephen. Foreshadowed in the first sentence of the book, this confidence reaches its peak with the advent of Bloom in the fourth chapter.

The introduction of Bloom into Joyce's fiction marks his movement from the fiction of solipsism to the novel-epic. With Bloom, a character so distant from the intellectual, artistic figure of Stephen, Joyce displays his confidence to treat "the other" objectively. Epistemologically Joyce should have no problems giving himself privileged access to Stephen's thoughts and actions in *A Portrait* and *Ulysses*, because Stephen is Joyce's recognized alter ego. But to treat Bloom in the same manner Joyce needs a technique that goes beyond simply placing a mirror up to himself.

It is no accident that Bloom appears in Joyce's fiction immediately after one of the most solipsistic passages in literature—Stephen's walk on the beach. In "Proteus" we are totally locked within Stephen's mind, seeing everything extending from him. But at this extreme limit of the fiction of solipsism Joyce breaks through to the portrayal of Bloom. Only by confronting solipsism can Joyce write *Ulysses*. Stephen's excessive concern with himself is a necessary step in the process moving beyond solipsism.

A move beyond solipsism is not, however, a move that eliminates subjectivity by erasing the subject. Joyce's "new objectivity" that allows the presentation of Bloom continues to account for the subject, since, as has often been noted, there is as much Joyce in Bloom as in Stephen. In fact, my persistent use of the terms *subjective* and *objective* to try to describe the effect of Joyce's techniques reveals how much our thinking is trapped in the type of thinking that the experience of reading *Ulysses* challenges. As Hugh Kenner puts it, the techniques of *Ulysses* move "beyond objectivity."[30] In *Ulysses*, it is the mirror-within-

30. See the last chapter of Kenner, *Joyce's Voices*, 64–99.

a-mirror technique, in which Joyce beholds himself, that frees the art-ist once again, like Shakespeare, to hold a mirror up to nature. So it is fitting that the culmination of all the mirror scenes finds Stephen and Bloom, those two mocking-mirror images of their creator, looking in a mirror and together regarding the face of William Shakespeare.

> (Stephen and Bloom gaze in the mirror. The face of William Shake-speare, beardless, appears there, rigid in facial paralysis, crowned by the reflection of the reindeer antlered hatrack in the hall.)
>
> SHAKESPEARE
>
> (In dignified ventriloquy.) 'Tis the loud laugh bespeaks the vacant mind. (To Bloom.) Thou thoughtest as how thou wastest invisible. Gaze. (He crows with a black capon's laugh.) Iagogo! How my Old-fellow chokit his Thursdaymomun. Iagogogo! (U 567.17–26)

But, as the allusion to Shakespeare reminds us, the movement beyond objectivity, including the image of the artist in the mirror that he places up to nature, is not "new" with Joyce. As Stephen painstakingly argues in the library, the same technique is to be found in Shake-speare's Renaissance plays. It is in Shakespeare's works that Joyce found a perfect model for his return to the world of his handiwork.

Chapter Two

Life, Love, Voyage Round Your Own Little World

Much has been written about Stephen's interpretation of Shakespeare, and much of what has been written tries to determine if Stephen's "practical criticism" of the plays implies an aesthetic different from his abstract theorizing in the last chapter of A Portrait. By writing on this topic again, I risk repeating work that has already been done. Nonetheless, I will risk repetition by asserting that I think there is a difference, a difference that critics' attention to minor distinctions too often causes them to overlook. In A Portrait, Stephen defends a theory of artistic impersonality in which the dramatic mode is considered the highest mode of art because it allows the artist to remain "invisible, refined out of existence, indifferent" (P 215); in Ulysses, Stephen constructs a theory in which the most famous dramatist in the English language makes a noticeable return to the world of his plays as a ghost. The artist, who has escaped in A Portrait in order to pare his fingernails, returns in Ulysses continually asserting the presence of his hidden hand at work—nails pared or not.

It is this ironic undercutting of the dramatic mode as the most impersonal that criticism overlooks when it relies on S. L. Goldberg's influential interpretation of Stephen's Shakespeare theory.[1] Goldberg argues, as I do, that Stephen's aesthetics have changed from A Portrait

1. See S. L. Goldberg, "Art and Freedom," in his The Classical Temper (London: Chatto & Windus, 1961), 66–99.

to *Ulysses*. But even though he considers Stephen's aesthetic theory in *A Portrait* to be flawed, Goldberg continues to argue for the superiority of the dramatic mode because of its objectivity. My argument is just the opposite. If we are to apply Stephen's Shakespeare theory to *Ulysses*—which I believe, along with Goldberg, we are invited to do—we do not have a justification for the continuation of the objective presentation of most of the chapters preceding "Scylla and Charybdis." What we have is a justification for Joyce's own return to the world of his text, as manifested in the increasingly noticeable styles of the second half. Joyce, like Turko the terrible, "*the boy / That can enjoy / Invisibility*" (*U* 10.4–6), makes gesture after gesture through his silent pantomime of printed signs to call attention to the artist's existence *within* the text. Like those algebraic symbols in "Nestor" that move across the page "in grave morrice, in the mummery of their letters" (*U* 28.11–12), the dark words of print in *Ulysses* in imitation of those dark men Averroës and Moses Maimonides flash in their "mocking mirrors the obscure soul of the world" (*U* 28.17). And it is by algebra, Buck has told us, that Stephen "proves" the return of Shakespeare to the world of his plays.

The dramatic mode of *Ulysses* does not simply imply that "the personality of the artist . . . refines itself out of existence, impersonalizes itself, so to speak" (*P* 215). Look, for instance, at "Circe," the only purely dramatic chapter in *Ulysses*. It has traditionally been called one of Joyce's most subjective episodes, and it has artist Shakespeare return in a central scene mockingly to reflect in a mirror the image of the book's two major characters.

At the same time, one of the rarely noticed ironies of Joyce's chapter about England's national playwright is that it is one of the least dramatic in the entire book. There is very little physical action until that grand performer Buck enters the scene. For the most part, the drama takes place within one person's mind—Stephen's. It is the drama of an internalized Socratic dialogue in which Stephen attempts to "jest on. Know thyself" (*U* 216.14). But as the title of Buck's play—*Everyman His own Wife or A Honeymoon in the Hand (a national immorality in three orgasms)* (*U* 216.35–38)—suggests, the "know" in the Socratic dictum can be read in the biblical sense. The quest for self-

knowledge runs the risk of indulging in self-enclosed subjectivity, a literary equivalent of masturbation. Stephen's performance, however, is
not self-indulgent subjectivity. As the play of the chapter shows, self-
knowledge for him comes in trying to understand another and then
trying to relate that understanding to an audience. That the other is
Shakespeare only adds to the chapter's mental drama. Stephen's theory accounts for Shakespeare's subjectivity in his art and, in doing so,
establishes Shakespeare's work as a model for *Ulysses*.[2]

It is common knowledge that the theory Joyce gives to Stephen
was once his own. It has also been established that the Shakespeare
theory was important for Joyce in composing *Ulysses*. The Shakespeare chapter of *Ulysses* was one of the first, if not the first, that
Joyce successfully completed. A letter that Joyce wrote to Ezra Pound
on 9 April 1917, in response to a request for excerpts for publication,
stated: "As regards excerpts from *Ulysses*, the only thing I could send
would be the Hamlet chapter, or part of it—which, however, would
suffer by excision." Furthermore, A. Walton Litz shows that, except
for the Telemachiad, "Scylla and Charybdis" was the first chapter
Joyce worked on. For instance, in the margin of Joyce's early manuscript of "Proteus," Joyce has written "A.E.I.O.U.," which appears in
"Scylla and Charybdis," indicating that he was gathering material for
the two at the same time.[3]

And there is another interesting set of dates. Ellmann tells us that
Joyce began to work out his Shakespeare theory during June, 1904 (*JJ*
161). Then in Trieste in 1912–1913, Joyce reworked his theory for a
series of thirteen lectures on *Hamlet* (*JJ* 355).[4] If indeed the Shakespeare theory is one of the seeds that leads to the birth of the book,
then the book has one of its origins in June, 1904. Another of the

2. Richard Ellmann, *The Consciousness of Joyce* (London: Faber & Faber, 1977), 45–72,
argues in a quite different manner that Shakespeare provided Joyce with a model for
the use of subjectivity in art.
3. Forrest Read (ed.), *Pound/Joyce* (New York: New Directions, 1970), 105; A. Walton Litz, *The Art of James Joyce* (New York: Oxford University Press, 1964), 142; see
the "Proteus" manuscript, V.A.3, in the Lockwood Memorial Library, State University
of New York at Buffalo.
4. See Richard Ellmann, *Ulysses on the Liffey* (New York: Oxford University Press,
1972), 81.

book's seeds is of course Joyce's first walk with Nora Barnacle, which supposedly took place 16 June 1904. Joyce could easily link his theory about Shakespeare's creative process with his encounter with Nora, just as Stephen links the writing of Shakespeare's plays with Shakespeare's encounter with Ann Hathaway. Furthermore, returning to his Shakespeare theory seems to have given Joyce the spark to conceive his new work. Work on *Ulysses* began a year after the Trieste lectures. Finally, when Joyce placed his Shakespeare chapter in *Ulysses*, he gave it the honored position of concluding the first half of the book's eighteen chapters. Joyce's late schema indicates the importance Joyce attached to "Scylla and Charybdis." Its organ is the brain; its art, literature. The brains of the book theorize on the enterprise of literature, specifically Joyce's enterprise in writing *Ulysses*. So, even if the *Shakespeare Quarterly* would reject Stephen's theory as too idiosyncratic, the *James Joyce Quarterly* might consider publishing it as the best piece of criticism on *Ulysses* yet written. It is an important part of the tale of the telling.

Stephen's Shakespeare theory both provides theoretical justification for the return of the artist to his handiwork and, in exposing Stephen's techniques of counterfeiting Shakespeare's London, lays bare some of the techniques Joyce uses to counterfeit his Dublin. Stephen, like Joyce, knows that he fabricates. "Don't tell them he was nine years old when [the star shining at Shakespeare's birth] was quenched" (*U* 210.15). Even so, he deliberately works to deceive his audience. "They list. And in the porches of their ears I pour" (*U* 196.38). Earlier Stephen, a fictional character, invokes Ignatius Loyola and "composition of place" (*U* 188.25) to make his fiction convincing. He identifies realism as the technique of his deception. "Local colour. Work in all you know. Make them accomplices" (*U* 188.19–20). In the next chapter, "Wandering Rocks," Joyce heeds his fictional character's advice by adopting composition of place to evoke the fictional Dublin in which Stephen himself wanders. And as we read these pages of one long gone we are reminded that realism, including local color, is also Joyce's technique for convincing his audience to believe his fiction entitled *Ulysses*.

Not only do both Joyce and Stephen achieve composition of place and local color, they use a similar method to do so. To re-create Shakespeare's London, Stephen relies on Charles W. Wallace's "New Shakespeare Discoveries: Shakespeare as a Man Among Men": "By reference to a map of London you will see that the Globe Theatre is situated on the south side of the Thames just between the Bankside and Maiden Lane, almost directly South of Silver Street. You can see Shakespeare start out from Silver Street for the theatre."[5] Stephen's sentence, "Shakespeare has left the huguenot's house in Silver Street and walks by the swanmews along the riverbank" (U 188.21–22), both echoes Wallace's second sentence and anticipates the type of sentence we encounter in "Wandering Rocks." "The superior, the very reverend John Conmee S. J., reset his smooth watch in his interior pocket as he came down the presbytery steps" (U 219.1–3). Equally revealing is the fact that Wallace relies on a map to re-create Shakespeare's London; Joyce's use of maps to re-create Dublin in fiction is well known. Today readers rely on the maps provided by Hart and Knuth in their own re-creation of Ulysses.

By having Stephen construct his theory with methods similar to the ones Joyce uses to create Ulysses, Joyce borrows a technique from the artist Stephen theorizes about. Just as Shakespeare may include a play within his plays, so Joyce uses "Scylla and Charybdis" as a fiction within a fiction. In the middle of the chapter, Stephen's performance is rendered in overtly dramatic form. In fact, Stephen's comment, "the play begins" (U 188.27), refers to his "play" in its many senses: Shakespeare's drama, Stephen's staged performance, and Joyce's fun.[6] All these aspects invite the reader to reflect on the nature of the work of art he is reading or watching.

In Shakespeare and the Idea of the Play, Anne Righter argues that the play within a play evolved when drama in the Renaissance became more and more autonomous, more and more cut off from direct audience participation.[7] She sees the play within a play as essentially a technique for maintaining contact with the audience. With characters in his

5. Don Gifford and Robert J. Seidman, Notes for Joyce (New York: E. P. Dutton, 1974), 165.
6. Hélène Cixous, The Exile of James Joyce, trans. Sally A. J. Purcell (New York: David Lewis, 1972), 564–95, makes a similar point about the "play" beginning. Her entire discussion of Stephen's aesthetic is provocative.
7. Anne Righter, Shakespeare and the Idea of the Play (London: Chatto & Windus, 1962), 83.

play acting as spectators to a play, the playwright can instruct the audience as to its role. In the case of *Hamlet*, the play that the characters watch happens to be a simplified example of the type of revenge tragedy that *Hamlet* could have turned into were it not for Hamlet's self-consciousness. In turn, Hamlet's self-consciousness is his awareness of the play on the word *act*. For him, to act, in this case to take revenge, is to act, that is, to play a role. Hamlet, then, becomes the ideal producer of the play, a role that allows him to explore the relations between art and reality.

The spectator is exposed to this complex relationship before Hamlet is. In his famous first speech Hamlet expresses the power of his grief for his dead father by distinguishing between real and mock grief. Responding to his uncle's and mother's questions, Hamlet indignantly announces that his grief is more than mere seeming. "Seems, madam? Nay, it is. I know not 'seems.'" Having observed the court's theatrical display of grief, Hamlet claims that his grief is much deeper. He renounces the "inky cloak" of mourning as nothing more than an external covering. Furthermore, Hamlet denies that even those seemingly unmistakable signs of personality, words and actions, can truly denote his grief. They are merely external manifestations of his feelings—mere appearances. "These indeed seem, / For they are actions that a man might play" (I.ii.76, 77, 83–84).

But if we remember that we are watching a play, the actor playing Hamlet undercuts the very words he speaks. Because Hamlet is not a real person but a product of Shakespeare's imagination, how else would we know Hamlet's grief or indeed Hamlet himself if it were not for the inky cloak of a text and an actor turning those marks of the poet's pen into "windy suspiration" (I.ii.79) and actions? So if we let ourselves believe that the actor in front of us feels real grief, we are brought face to face with the fact that it is his skill as an actor, at "seeming," that makes us believe so. And it would take an even more subtle actor (or a poor one) to convince us that Hamlet is merely "seeming," putting on a show for devious purposes. By the time of the play within the play, Hamlet has learned the importance of "playing." "The play's the thing" with which Hamlet hopes to evoke a guilty response from the king.

Stephen's Shakespeare theory produces effects similar to Hamlet's "play." By having Stephen construct a fiction within a work of fiction, Joyce can comment on the nature of fiction making. Furthermore, by showing us the reaction of Stephen's audience, he can instruct his audience on roles it might and might not adopt in reading *Ulysses*. Finally, just as Hamlet's self-consciousness is his awareness of "acting" as the basis of all our actions, so Stephen's is the awareness of the fictional base of our construction of the world. The world is founded on the void of incertitude, the possibly "legal fiction" of fatherhood; from birth on, our lives are conditioned by many kinds of fictions. Moreover, the world is written by a playwright. "The playwright who wrote the folio of this world" (*U* 213.20−21), like Shakespeare, created a world out of his own image. He "is doubtless all in all in all of us" (*U* 213.23−24). Stephen's fiction within the larger fiction of *Ulysses* offers us one more mirror within a mirror in which a chapter reflects the book at large and in which fictions reflect their creators and their creators are reflections of fictions.

According to Stephen, Shakespeare's plays will always be in one sense a mirror of their creator. He populates his world by giving birth to characters made in his own image. In the plays, "the boy of act one is the mature man of act five. All in all. In *Cymbeline*, in *Othello* he is bawd and cuckold. He acts and is acted on. Lover of an ideal or a perversion, like José he kills the real Carmen. His unremitting intellect is the hornmad Iago ceaselessly willing that the moor in him shall suffer" (*U* 212.30−35).

Need I add that what Stephen has to say about Shakespeare also applies to Joyce? In writing *Ulysses*, Joyce repeats Shakespeare's act of populating his artistic world with doubles of himself. From the first-person narrator of the childhood stories in *Dubliners* to Little Chandler to Gabriel Conroy to Stephen to Bloom, Joyce's characters often mirror aspects of their creator. Presiding over his artistic world as lord and giver of life, Joyce can defy the historical world that limits him to one and only one ineluctably preconditioned self. In the historical world the only possible James Joyce is the actual James Joyce, but in his fiction, there is an infinite number of James Joyces as he weaves and unweaves his image in his work. He is teacher, lawyer, medical student (isn't Buck's demythologizing wit also an aspect of former medical student Joyce?), journalist, artist, father, son, and even mother. Like God, like Shakespeare, Joyce reveals himself in his creation. He too is all in all.

Stephen's theory lays bare yet another technique by which Joyce / Shakespeare return to participate in their creations. "He has hidden his own name, a fair name, William, in the plays, a super here, a clown there, as a painter of old Italy set his face in a dark corner of his canvas" (*U* 209.32–34). In *Ulysses*, there are some interesting Jameses. For instance, while in search of a novel for Molly, Bloom comes across *Fair Tyrants*. The name of the book's author is James Lovebirch; our hidden forger seems to anticipate the outcry against *Ulysses* as cheap pornography by giving his own first name to Lovebirch, a pseudonym commonly used in the type of flagellation literature that appeals to Bloom. Likewise, in "Circe," Joyce attaches his first name to the name Pidgeon (*U* 520.29). Earlier "*le sacré pigeon*" has been suggested as the solution to the mystery of Christ's paternity. "Jimmy Pidgeon" is a figure for the Creator. Then, toward the end of "Oxen of the Sun" Joyce claims authorship of the whole soupy mess of parodies with the phrase "Bovril, by James" (*U* 427.19). Finally, as Molly spins the web of her soliloquy she remarks, "I don't like books with a Molly in them like that one he brought me about the one from Flanders" (*U* 756.24–25). But thereafter she pleads, "O Jamesy let me up out of this pooh sweets of sin" (*U* 769.31–32). If the reader has read the signatures in front of him carefully, he catches the author in the act of being addressed by one of the characters in his book, just as Joyce once dreamed of Molly talking to him.[8]

Joyce doesn't make his presence felt merely by hiding his name in his text. As has long been observed, he populates *Ulysses* with the names of characters from his earlier works. Gabriel Conroy, Mrs. Sin-

---

8. In *The Annotated Lolita*, by Vladimir Nabokov, edited, with preface, introduction, and notes, by Alfred Appel, Jr. (New York: McGraw-Hill, 1970), xxv, Appel first pointed out this way of reading Molly's comment. James Van Dyck Card, "'Contradicting': The Word for Joyce's 'Penelope,'" *James Joyce Quarterly*, XI (Fall, 1973), 26, mistakenly attributes this discovery to Nabokov himself. How this comment works on the naturalistic level is explained by the use of the Irish "Jamesy" for "Jaysus."

ico, Mrs. Riordan, and others are mentioned. Bob Doran and Lenehan reappear, renewing their fictional life that began in *Dubliners*. Because we have met these characters before in fictions written by James Joyce, their presence serves to remind us that we are reading a book written by the author with that same name. Joyce even includes the titles *Chamber Music* (*U* 282.27) and Dubliners (*U* 145.2) within the pages of *Ulysses*. In fact, the latter occurs immediately before Stephen tells his parable of the plums, a tale provocatively suggestive of "The Sisters," the first story in *Dubliners*, also about two old ladies puckered by their prunelike life in Dublin. Perhaps we are witnessing Joyce portraying Stephen with the "seed" for that story, although eventually this seed was spewed out in favor of a more effective version.

Finally the forger of *Ulysses* virtually confesses his crime by affixing his initials to his handiwork. Throughout "Cyclops," O'Molloy's last name is dropped and he is referred to as J.J. If we read simply according to the precepts of naturalism, when O'Molloy speaks we hear a minor figure in a work of fiction speaking. But read as part of the tale of the telling, O'Molloy speaks as "J. J.," the creator who, as Stephen says, "is doubtless all in all in all of us" (*U* 213.23–24). In fact, like Little Chandler and Gabriel Conroy, O'Molloy is another example of what Joyce might have become. The portrait of O'Molloy could easily describe Joyce if he had stayed in Dublin and pursued a legal career. Having once been the "cleverest fellow at the junior bar," he has maintained his cultivated appearance, but lost his practice to a weakness for gambling. A "wellread fellow," "he does some literary work for the *Express* with Gabriel Conroy" (*U* 125.18, 17). "His forte in both 'Aeolus' and 'Cyclops' is the quip that goes unnoticed,"[9] and, like Joyce, he seems especially knowledgeable about libel cases (*U* 322). Ellmann says of O'Molloy's creator that "the image of himself making a public self-defense with the eloquence of Seymour Bushe and John F. Taylor never quite left Joyce" (*JJ* 207). Sure enough, it is J.J. who quotes Bushe's famous defense of Bloom in "Circe": "I would deal in

9. David Hayman, "Cyclops," in Clive Hart and David Hayman (eds.), *James Joyce's "Ulysses"* (Berkeley: University of California Press, 1974), 256 (Hayman's phrase). It is also interesting that "J. J." is stamped on the front cover of the "Cyclops" manuscript, V.A.8 Copybook, in the Lockwood Memorial Library.

especial with atavism. There have been cases of shipwreck and somnambulism in my client's family. If the accused could speak he could a
tale unfold one of the strangest that have ever been narrated between
the covers of a book" (*U* 463.18–22). Once again Joyce draws attention to the fact that we are reading a book. The strange tale that
Bloom could unfold is, of course, "this chaffering allincluding most far-
raginous chronicle" (*U* 423.26) that we hold in our hands. This reference to atavism adds even another dimension to Bloom's defense. As
only Joyce or the reader could know, Bloom is indeed an avatar whose
ancestors have cases of shipwreck (Odysseus) and somnambulism
(Hamlet's ghost) in their history. So, speaking in "*dignified ventriloquy*"
(*U* 567.22) through one of his characters, puppet master Joyce can
defend his hero Bloom, all the while adding to the "rebutting evidence" that J.J. claims will "prove up to the hilt that the hidden hand is
again at its old game" (*U* 464.11–12). In turn, Bloom calls J. J. O'Molloy
what he is—"a mighthavebeen" (*U* 125.13).

Signaled by Stephen's theory to look for reflections of the artist
within his creation, we find them everywhere. Furthermore, just as
Stephen constructs the history of Shakespeare's art as one of escape
and return, so we are invited to see Joyce's art conforming to the
same pattern. And not only do Shakespeare's and Joyce's art adhere to
a return story pattern, so do their lives; the patterns of art and life
repeat one another with a difference.

Shakespeare's life repeats a pattern of escape and return. Stripped
of his sexual confidence by Ann's premature seduction of him in a rye
field, Shakespeare avoids confrontation with Ann and her sexual ag-
gressiveness, which suggests extramarital sexual experience, by escaping to London. There he turns to art and creates imaginary characters
for his plays rather than breeding children. His plays are "the creation
he has piled up to hide him from himself" (*U* 197.8–9). While writing
his plays, he substitutes whores for wives. "Twenty years he dallied
there between conjugal love and its chaste delights and scortatory
love and its foul pleasures" (*U* 201.29–31). Meanwhile, back in Stratford, his two brothers, Richard and Edmund, are busy cuckolding him.
Finally, Shakespeare leaves London and "returns after a life of absence
to that spot of earth where he was born, where he has always been,
man and boy, a silent witness and there, his journey of life ended, he

plants his mulberrytree in the earth. Then dies. The motion is ended" (U 213.1–4).

As Stephen points out, this pattern of escape and return is repeated in Shakespeare's art. The escape is chronicled in the early poems and plays. *Venus and Adonis* grows out of Shakespeare's seduction by Ann. The wound to his sexual self-confidence caused by this seduction is recorded in the sonnets. Then Shakespeare documents his escape from Ann and Stratford in the early plays, which sound their note of banishment. Ann's continued sexual ascendancy over her husband results in the creation of the dominant female figures of Cleopatra and Cressida. But with the great tragedies, especially *Hamlet*, Shakespeare reverses his escapist tendency and turns to confront himself and his situation. Finally, the late plays signal Shakespeare's return and reconciliation.

While Shakespeare's plays can be seen as a fictional world to which he escapes in order to avoid confrontation with the disappointments of life, they can also be seen as the mirror forcing him to confront those aspects of his life from which he is trying to escape. This is because an artist cannot help but portray personal concerns in his art. His art helps him, as Mallarmé said of Hamlet, to learn to read the book of himself. Yet the book of himself that the artist has written is not merely a representation of Shakespeare's life. It also helps shape the life it mirrors. The act of writing could be said to have created Shakespeare, as well as vice versa. It is through his art that he sets in motion the return his plays record.

Similarly, in *Ulysses* it is Stephen's working out of his Shakespeare theory, in which the Shakespeare created is in some ways a mirror image of himself, that sets in motion the book's movement toward return. At the end of the chapter, Stephen sights the two plumes of smoke that he associates with Shakespeare's *Cymbeline* and its harmonious ending and that for Odysseus signal a return to Ithaca. It is at this point in the book that Joyce, having given himself theoretical justification for the return of the artist to his handiwork, embarks on his odyssey of return that unfolds in the second half of the book. *Ulysses* is indeed Joyce's *Hamlet*, as it marks the return of the artist to the world of his creation, just as Shakespeare returns to *Hamlet* as the ghost.

It is Stephen's identification of the ghost of Hamlet *père* as a figure for Shakespeare returning to his artistic world that is the most idio-syncratic contribution of his theory. Drawing on the old tradition that Shakespeare acted the role of the ghost in *Hamlet*, Stephen alters the normal autobiographical reading of the play and contends that Shake-speare, like God as the Holy Ghost, returns as a voice to the world he has created: "He is a ghost, a shadow now, the wind by Elsinore's rocks or what you will, the sea's voice, a voice heard only in the heart of him who is the substance of his shadow, the son consubstantial with the father" (*U* 197.12–15).

Stephen's identification of the returning artist as the ghost of the father, rather than the son, might help settle a long critical contro-versy over how closely author Joyce should be equated with the son of his right hand, character Stephen. Just as critics of the nineteenth cen-tury, intent on reading Shakespeare's plays autobiographically, insisted on identifying Shakespeare as Hamlet *fils*, so twentieth-century critics continue to identify Joyce with Stephen. Indeed, as Stephen admits, the son (Hamlet / Stephen) does share a special relation to his creator (Shakespeare / Joyce), just as Christ does to God, but his relationship is a mysterious one.

The nature of that relationship is hinted at by Stephen's obsessive concern with the Arian and Sabellian heresies. If we dwell for a mo-ment on Stephen's comparison of the Holy Trinity to an artistic trinity, we soon see that Stephen is not Joyce, as Christ is not God. The re-lationship of the son to his creator remains as inexplicable as the mystery of the Holy Trinity. Father (Joyce) and son (Stephen) have a mysterious connection: they even share the same essence, but have a distinct personality. Trying to explain the relation of the creator to his counterfeit autobiographical figure, Stephen, critics succumb to two heresies. The Arian heresy claims that father and son are separate and distinct; the Sabellian heresy claims that father and son are one and the same.[10] Both heresies distort the mysterious relationship, because the creator of *Ulysses*, like God, is both inside and outside his creation,

10. For discussions of the heresies, see William T. Noon, S.J., *Joyce and Aquinas* (New Haven: Yale University Press, 1957); Robert Boyle, S.J., "Mystery," in Louis Bonnerot (ed.), *"Ulysses": Cinquante Ans Après* (Paris: Didier, 1972), 243–61; Robert Kellogg, "Scylla and Charybdis," in Hart and Hayman (eds.), *James Joyce's "Ulysses,"* 168–69.

seeming to manifest himself as both immanent and transcendent, escaping only to return and returning only to escape.

But while Joyce's return as son has long been recognized, his return, like Shakespeare, as a ghost is not so obvious—nor should it be, given the nature of ghosts. Nonetheless, the ghostly presence of creator Joyce presiding over his creation is everywhere felt or, should we say, heard. Just as Shakespeare returns to *Hamlet* as the voice of the ghost, so Joyce calls attention to his return through the increasingly obtrusive narrative voices that dominate the second half of the book. It is through these stylistic capers that Joyce finds a way to haunt the world of *Ulysses*.

Joyce, however, is not one to establish such an intricate parallel between himself and Shakespeare without suggesting even more detailed correspondences. One continues to wonder whether Joyce did not create a figure to correspond to the ghost of Hamlet *père*, whether he too does not send a ghostlike figure of the artist to return to haunt the world of Dublin that might have forgotten him, "a silent witness" who "returns after a life of absence to that spot of earth where he was born, where he has always been, man and boy" (*U* 213.1–3). With Stephen we might wonder, "Where's the third person of the Blessed Trinity?" (*U* 595.20–21) Or as Stephen poses the question elsewhere, letting his audience supply the answer: "What is a ghost? Stephen said with tingling energy. One who has faded into impalpability through death, through absence, through change of manners. Elizabethan London lay as far from Stratford as corrupt Paris lies from virgin Dublin. Who is the ghost from *limbo patrum*, returning to the world that has forgotten him? Who is king Hamlet?" (*U* 188.6–11)

As Joyce knew all too well, the best way for an author to be remembered is to create questions, such as "Who is king Hamlet?" and to leave them unanswered. Ellmann quotes him as saying, "I've put in so many enigmas and puzzles that it will keep the professors busy for centuries arguing over what I meant, and that's the only way of insuring one's immortality" (*JJ* 535). At the risk of becoming one of those busy professors Joyce loved to mock, I would like to suggest that the way in which Joyce contrived to haunt *Ulysses* is through one of the most famous of all the enigmas of *Ulysses*. It may well be that we are given a hint of the answer to "Who is king Hamlet?" by a question that five hundred pages later echoes Stephen's, a question that Joyce delighted in asking American readers of the text in Paris, a question that countless critics have tried to answer. Who is King Hamlet? Who is M'Intosh?

If Joyce did decide to return ghostlike to the Dublin where he was born, the cemetery of "Hades" would be a good choice, cemeteries being the traditional hangout for ghosts. Appropriately, at Paddy Dignam's funeral the "lankylooking galoot" (*U* 109.29) in the macintosh pops out of nowhere, in between Bloom's thoughts of "Have you ever seen a ghost?" (*U* 108.10–11) and "If we were all suddenly somebody else" (*U* 110.24). As M'Intosh, Joyce, a rather lanky-looking fellow himself, could preside over the death of one of his own characters, just as M'Intosh later presides as a silent witness over the cavalcade of characters at the end of "Wandering Rocks." When Dignam loses his identity while being laid to rest in a brown mortuary habit, M'Intosh is provided with both coat and (mis)identity and starts to haunt Bloom's imagination. Ironically, while Odysseus descends to Hades to make the spirit of Tiresias speak, Bloom in his journey to Hades does not even recognize the spirit of his book's prophet.[11]

M'Intosh's appearances in "Hades" marks the presence of the book's creator in another important way. Through "Hades" the book's narrative technique has tried to approach an objective rendition of the action. As Culler says, the book's language cannot be easily recuperated as the speech of a characterizable narrator. The narrator, if one exists, has remained invisible, refined out of existence. But in the very next chapter, a set of obtrusive headlines begins to disrupt the objec-

11. See Shari Benstock, "Ulysses as Ghoststory," *James Joyce Quarterly*, XII (Summer, 1975), 396–413, for another account of *Ulysses* as a ghost story. She also implies that M'Intosh is Joyce. Alfred Appel has maintained this theory for years and first suggested it to me. Lynn De Vore, "A Final Note on M'Intosh," *James Joyce Quarterly*, XVI (Spring, 1979), 347–50, makes an argument similar to mine in content, but with far too much certainty about her ability to pin down the identity of a man with no name. Stuart Gilbert, *James Joyce's "Ulysses"* (New York: Random House, 1955), 170–73, argues that M'Intosh's Homeric double is Theoclymenos. But Odysseus descends into Hades to see Tiresias, not Theoclymenos.

tive style. By appearing in the chapter before "Aeolus" and then again at the end of "Wandering Rocks," just before the flagrant style of "Sirens," M'Intosh helps announce the resurrection of the spirit presiding over the creation of the book. If in recent years we have experienced the death of the author, his death does not rule out the possibility that he can return to haunt the world he has created.

The Resurrection motif surrounding M'Intosh is not one I have manufactured. It is so pervasive that Robert Adams Day has tried to identify M'Intosh as the risen Christ.[12] Such an identification would not rule out the M'Intosh / Joyce connection, since Joyce enjoyed playing the role of the suffering Christ as well as others. He had some confirmation of this role in life, since his first return to Dublin from Paris included travel on Easter Sunday, having been prompted by a telegram he received on Good Friday, 1903: "MOTHER DYING COME HOME FATHER" (JJ 133). His return eventually led to a visit in mourning to the cemetery where M'Intosh makes his appearance. In "Cyclops" we are told, "The man in the brown macintosh loves a lady who is dead" (U 333.32–33).

M'Intosh, then, as the spirit of his creator, returning to the world of his creation in the cemetery, only to refine himself once more out of an existence, temporarily to enjoy a state of invisibility. As Bloom thinks of M'Intosh: "Didn't hear. What? Where has he disappeared to? Not a sign. Well of all the. Has anybody here seen? Kay ee double ell. Become invisible. Good Lord, what became of him?" (U 112.13–15). And just to make sure that the identification of M'Intosh with the "Good Lord" of Ulysses is not without further textual support, let me add, as others have before me, that El is Hebrew for God and that in the cabalistic tradition K and ll are symbolic of the resurrection. When M'Intosh is resurrected later in the day, the macintosh he is wearing adds a k; when Bloom appears with M'Intosh in the Evening Telegraph, he has lost an l, making him Boom—a noise in the street, or God (U 427.17, 647.41).

12. Robert Adams Day, "Joyce's Waste Land and Eliot's Unknown God," in Eric Rothstein (ed.), Literary Monographs, IV (Madison: University of Wisconsin Press, 1971), 172. Day's study is one of the most thorough available, though he and I make different guesses about M'Intosh's identity.

It is interesting to note that the creator of *Ulysses*, while writing his country's national epic in exile in Zurich, was known to wear a brown overcoat. Frank Budgen reports meeting Joyce on Bahnhofstrasse, "the brown overcoat buttoned up to his chin."[13] In a letter Joyce describes his coat as "shellcocoacoloured" (*Letters*, *I* 85). If the coat's epithet is in *Ulysses* (*U* 45.41–46.1), maybe the coat is as well. In fact, this could be the coat Joyce wore in the photograph serving as a model for the cover of the 1969 Viking Compass edition of *Dubliners*, in which Joyce, attired in a long overcoat, is shown surveying the Dublin to which he returned artistically, if not actually.

M'Intosh's similarities to the ghost of Hamlet *père* are reinforced when he is mentioned in "Oxen of the Sun." Although the muddled slang that ends the chapter provides him with another cover, we do learn that, like King Hamlet, he has woman problems—"man all tattered and torn that married a maiden all forlorn. Slung her hook, she did" (*U* 427.23–24)—and has become a lonely walker, "walking Mackintosh of lonely canyon" (*U* 427.24–25).

When M'Intosh appears in the next chapter, "Circe," he enters, as all stage ghosts must, through a trapdoor. For a minor character in a work of fiction, the man in the macintosh exhibits unusual knowledge of its main character. Pointing an *"elongated finger"* (*U* 485.9) at Bloom (are the nails well pared?), he undercuts Bloom's masquerade as Lord Mayor of Bloomusalem by calling him a liar and revealing his mother's maiden name, Higgins. M'Intosh goes so far as to rename the man who gave him his misnomer with his own pseudonym. "That man is Leopold M'Intosh, the notorious fireraiser" (*U* 485.11–12).

Although M'Intosh soon disappears, he resurfaces in a new role at the brothel. When Bloom arrives at Bella's, *"on the antlered rack of the hall hang a man's hat and waterproof"* (*U* 502.4–5). This is the same antlered rack that will crown the image of Shakespeare's head in the mirror. In the brothel, Lynch sets the scene: "Enter a ghost and hobgoblins" (*U* 503.7). Sure enough, the ghost of Bloom's grandfather Virag, wearing a brown macintosh, comes falling down the "chimneyflue" (*U* 511.22). Virag also turns out to be extremely knowledgeable

13. Frank Budgen, *James Joyce and the Making of "Ulysses"* (Bloomington: Indiana University Press, 1960), 19.

about the book in which he appears. After scientifically describing the scene in the brothel, he makes a number of remarks that have unsettlingly obvious application to *Ulysses*. Virag is careful to point out the book's meticulous realism, "Observe the attention to details of dustspecks" (*U* 512.20). Bloom gets into the act and reflects that "it has been an unusually fatiguing day, a chapter of accidents" (*U* 514.12–13). Next Virag is allowed to sum up *Ulysses*' encyclopedic nature, "This book tells you how to act with all descriptive particulars" (*U* 514.26–27), and Joyce's parodic style, "From the sublime to the ridiculous is but a step" (*U* 515.2–3). Finally, if we are still confused, Virag advises: "For all these knotty points see the seventeenth book of my Fundamentals of Sexology or the Love Passion which Doctor L. B. says is the book sensation of the year" (*U* 515.28–30). It is "Ithaca," the seventeenth chapter of *Ulysses*, whose scientific catechism tries to answer many questions raised in this "book sensation of the year" and, in doing so, raises many others, including "Who was M'Intosh?"[14]

The identity of the one who poses these and other knotty points for both readers and characters is suggested shortly after Virag's appearance, with the arrival of Philip Drunk and Philip Sober, "*two Oxford dons with lawnmowers. . . . Both are masked with Matthew Arnold's face*" (*U* 518.17–19). Philip Drunk suspects, "I was here before. When was it not Atkinson his card I have somewhere? Mac somebody. Unmack I have it. He told me about, hold on, Swinburne, was it, no?" (*U* 519.1–4). The answer to this unanswered riddle, the Mac somebody like Atkinson, might be F. M'Curdy Atkinson (*U* 216.7) but might also be Mackintosh.

The spirit of M'Intosh pervades the book. He is capable of appearing and disappearing at will, and his appearances and disappearances are always suggestive. As a Joycean sleuth says of him, "He gathers many of the archetypal themes of the novel around himself. Number thirteen at the funeral, he is Christ or Judas. Wandering through Dublin, he is Odysseus or the Wandering Jew. Popping up from graveyards and trap doors he is Satan ('Where the deuce did he pop out of?' [*U* 110.11–12]); or Christ resurrected. Sliding down the chimney, he is

14. Appel (ed.), *The Annotated Lolita*, xxv, mentions Virag's comment, "That suits your book, eh?" (*U* 513.27)

God, or Christ descended. As a ruined man, he is Adam. As an apparition he is Hamlet's ghost. As the lover of a dead lady, he is Dante."[15]

What better answer than "Joyce" do we have to the question that raises the "selfinvolved enigma": Who was M'Intosh? (U 729.20, 23). No other character in the book so nicely fits the multiple roles that Stephen attributes to author Shakespeare: M'Intosh is truly "all in all."

But lacking a proper name, M'Intosh is also Noman, that role played so effectively by wily Odysseus to keep his identity hidden from the Cyclops. Unlike Odysseus, however, M'Intosh never cries out to reveal his true identity. As I will argue, M'Intosh's silence plays havoc with any attempt to pin down his identity with certainty. But it is also that silence that could provide Joyce with the perfect means to play the role of Shakespeare as the ghost in order to return as a silent witness to haunt the world of Ulysses. Aware of what keeps an author immortal, Joyce remains, like C. P. M'Coy and Stephen Dedalus, B.A., at Dignam's funeral, "conspicuous, needless to say, by [his] total absence (to say nothing of M'Intosh)" (U 648.2–4).

Joyce, however, is not the only figure in the book who is conspicuous by his absence. The figure who shares with him and Shakespeare the honor of having his name decorate the book's title page (the publisher was Shakespeare & Co.) is also everywhere felt but nowhere to be seen within the text. Any attempt to document the return story pattern, which Stephen offers as the pattern of Shakespeare's life and art and which Joyce self-consciously repeats in his life and art, cannot fail to mention Ulysses, the character who gives the Western world its archetypal return story pattern.

Confronted with a book whose title character never appears, critics have mustered all sorts of energy to make meaning of Ulysses' absence by pointing out minute correspondences between the action of the Odyssey and Ulysses. But it is important to remember that Joyce was first attracted to the hero Odysseus because of the universality of

15. Robert Crosman, "The Man in the Macintosh," James Joyce Quarterly, VI (Winter, 1968), 135. Crosman also associates M'Intosh with the Holy Ghost because of Bloom's reference to him in "Hades" (U 112.14–15): "Is there a buried allusion to the trinity here? If so, the Father is 'El' Bloom, the thunderer, Christ is 'the man who wasn't there,' the 'real M'Coy,' and M'Intosh is the Holy Ghost" (136).

his story, the everyman quality. What the *Odyssey* describes is the universal pattern of the return story: a character who has left home spends the rest of his life overcoming barriers, trying to return. The pattern of escape and return that Stephen weaves for Shakespeare's life and art is merely one repetition of the Odyssean pattern. And even though Stephen, so intent on playing the role of Hamlet *fils*, remains blind to the Odyssean parallels that cast him in the role of another son—Telemachus—Joyce leaves plenty of clues for the attentive reader to detect.

For instance, the only two times Ulysses is mentioned by name within the pages of the book occur in the chapter on Shakespeare.[16] First Stephen compares the events of *Lear*, *Othello*, *Hamlet*, and *Troilus and Cressida* to the *Odyssey*—"What softens the heart of a man, Shipwrecked in storms dire, Tried, like another Ulysses, Pericles, prince of Tyre?" (*U* 195.13–14)—and then Eglinton remarks that Shakespeare "puts Bohemia on the seacoast and makes Ulysses quote Aristotle" (*U* 212.1–2). (*Ulysses* certainly does quote its share of Aristotle.) So while Stephen misses the Odyssean echo when he refers to Hamlet as "the absentminded begger" (*U* 187.22), the reader might remember that this is the role Odysseus plays when he returns to Ithaca. Eglinton goes so far as to give Stephen a perfect opportunity to refer to the *Odyssey*. "Antiquity mentions famous beds, Second Eglinton puckered, bedsmiling. Let me think" (*U* 204.3–4). But Stephen turns the subject back to Aristotle, forgetting a more appropriate Greek.

Although Stephen will never see that the pattern of Shakespeare's life repeats the Odyssean archetype, his blindness allows the reader to see that just as Odysseus is forced to leave Ithaca, so Shakespeare is forced to leave Stratford. The twenty years that Shakespeare lingers in London away from home parallel the twenty years Odysseus wanders around the Mediterranean. In these twenty years, both indulge in extramarital sexual activities—Shakespeare with the whores of London and Odysseus with Calypso and Circe. Joyce reinforces the parallel between the two by having Stephen refer to Ann as Shakespeare's not-so-faithful Penelope. "But all those twenty years what do you

16. Ulysses occurs also as a first name: "Ulysses Browne of Camus" (*U* 330.18) and "Ulysses Grant" (*U* 757.10).

suppose poor Penelope in Stratford was doing behind the diamond panes?" (*U* 202.7–8)

Assigning Shakespeare twenty years in London seems to be another conscious fabrication by Joyce to make the myths of his two heroes coincide. In his notes for "Scylla and Charybdis" (V.A. 4, in the Lockwood Memorial Library), Joyce lists a number of dates for Shakespeare's life. But, using these dates, I could not make Shakespeare's absence from Stratford add up to twenty years.

The plots become even closer when we learn that Shakespeare, like Odysseus, takes revenge on his Penelope's suitors. Shakespeare, however, creates plays as his means of revenging himself on the forces that betrayed him in Stratford. In forming a world that he can manipulate and control, he revenges himself on Ann's suitors, his brothers Richard and Edmund, by turning them into villains on the stage. Furthermore, by returning as the ghost in *Hamlet*, to seek revenge on Claudius, Shakespeare imitates Odysseus, who returns like a ghost from the past to slay Penelope's suitors.

If Stephen remains blind to the fact that the pattern of escape and return he weaves is a variation of the *Odyssey* and if Stephen remains caught in an endless path of quest and escape that seems to promise no return, Joyce, nonetheless, allows him intellectually to recognize the importance of the return story pattern. Playing perfect fifths on the pianola in the magical world of "Circe," Stephen expounds for the benefit of Lynch's cap.

STEPHEN

Here's another for you. (*He frowns.*) The reason is because the fundamental and the dominant are separated by the greatest possible interval which . . .

THE CAP

Which? Finish. You can't.

STEPHEN

(*With an effort.*) Interval which. Is the greatest possible ellipse. Consistent with. The ultimate return. The octave. Which.

THE CAP

Which?
(*Outside the gramophone begins to blare* The Holy City.)

STEPHEN

(*Abruptly.*) What went forth to the ends of the world to traverse not itself. God, the sun, Shakespeare, a commercial traveller, having itself traversed in reality itself, becomes that self. Wait a moment. Wait a second. Damn that fellow's noise in the street. Self which it itself was ineluctably preconditioned to become. *Ecco!* (*U* 504.20—505.7)

The dominant-tonic interval describes the pattern of the greatest possible ellipse consistent with the ultimate return to the tonic. Stephen realizes that to achieve self-understanding one must wander as far as possible from the tonic, until he is finally compelled to return to the tonic, where he confronts the self he was preconditioned to become. God's journey to the world of his creation as Christ, the Son, followed by his return to himself; the journey of the sun around the earth; the journey of Shakespeare from Stratford to London and back; and the journey of a commercial traveler (Bloom) in the course of *Ulysses* all conform to this pattern, and so does Joyce's composition of the book in which Stephen and Bloom appear. At the end of his dialogue, Stephen receives affirmation of his insight from God in the form of a noise in the street.

In *Ulysses* the return story pattern becomes so inclusive that everything and everybody seem to return, from musical intervals to Shakespeare to God. Small segments and large segments are structured by a return. For instance, Bloom's entire day is mirrored in a miniature odyssey in "Calypso." Within his first chapter, Bloom leaves 7 Eccles Street, wanders the streets a bit, and returns. In the next chapter, he buys a piece of soap that has its own odyssey by moving from pocket to pocket.[17] But it is not until "Eumaeus," the chapter that starts the book's *Nostos* ("Return") and that corresponds to Odysseus' return to Ithaca, that the pervasiveness of the return story pattern is self-consciously revealed.

In "Eumaeus," Joyce anticipates a technique of *Finnegans Wake* by providing a catalogue of story after story that adheres to the Odyssean pattern. Return stories unify the events of the entire chapter.[18] In

17. See George H. Gibson, "The Odyssey of Leopold Bloom's Bar of Soap," *Furman Studies*, XIII (May, 1966), 16—19.
18. See James H. Maddox, *Joyce's "Ulysses" and the Assault upon Character* (New Brunswick: Rutgers University Press, 1978), 156—66.

the shelter Bloom and Stephen listen to the sailor D. B. Murphy telling tales of his own return to Ireland that day. Murphy sailed into Dublin on the highly symbolic three-masted schooner *Rosevean*, sighted by Stephen at the end of "Proteus," an event immediately preceding the arrival of Bloom in Joyce's literary world. After sailing, Odysseus-like, around the world, Murphy talks of reuniting with his wife. "She's my own true wife I haven't seen for seven years now, sailing about" (*U* 624.21–22).

Murphy's story and Bloom's own impending return to Molly cause Bloom to list stories with a similar theme. "Quite a number of stories there were on that particular Alice Ben Bolt topic, Enoch Arden and Rip van Winkle and does anybody hereabouts remember Caoc O'Leary, a favourite and most trying declamation piece, by the way, of poor John Casey and a bit of perfect poetry in its own small way?" (*U* 624.26–31). All of Bloom's allusions refer to variations on the *Odyssey* theme. Ben Bolt, a sailor who was away for twenty years, returns to find everything changed. Tennyson's hero Enoch Arden, shipwrecked, returns after ten years to find his wife married to his best friend. Resolving never to reveal himself, he conceals his return until his death. Rip van Winkle, acted by Bloom in a game of charades (*U* 377.25), falls asleep for twenty years and wakes up to find, like Ben Bolt, the world totally changed. Caoc O'Leary, from the poem "Caoc the Piper" by John Keegan (mistaken by Bloom for John Keegan Casey), returns after a twenty-year absence singing, "Does anybody hereabouts / Remember Caoc the Piper?" The common feature of all these stories is the return of someone after a long period of time—usually twenty years—to a world that may have forgotten him. As if these are not examples enough, Bloom goes on to mention a group of wandering sailors: Coleridge's ancient mariner, Sinbad the Sailor, and the hero of *The Flying Dutchman* (*U* 636.17, 33–37). "Mind you, I'm not saying that it's all a pure invention, he resumed. Analogous scenes are occasionally, if not often, met with" (*U* 636.22–24).

Alerted by the language of "Eumaeus," we can move beyond the chapter itself and link up with the returning-savior motif alluded to throughout *Ulysses*. Pamphlets are handed out announcing J. Alexander Dowie's proclamation of the coming of Elijah. In "Aeolus," Professor MacHugh refers to Moses, who led the Jews on a return to the promised land. And Stephen's analogy of the artist with God in "Scylla and Charybdis," plus numerous other allusions, emphasizes the return of God to his world in the body of Christ, the Savior.

Elijah, Moses, and Christ, however, are not merely fictional characters. Although enshrouded in myth, their stories depend upon the reader's belief in their historical existence. So having included fictional as well as mythical and religious figures in its inventory of returning heroes, "Eumaeus" also lists historical characters. A nationalistic cabman turns the conversation in the shelter to Parnell, who he believes will return to save the country. "One morning you would open the paper, the cabman affirmed, and read, *Return of Parnell*. He bet them what they liked. A Dublin fusilier was in that shelter one night and said he saw him in South Africa" (*U* 648.42–649.2). At Paddy Dignam's funeral Mr. Power had suggested the same possibility: "Some say he is not in that grave at all. That the coffin was filled with stones. That one day he will come again" (*U* 112.40–41). Nowhere before in Joyce's fiction had anyone entertained the possibility of Parnell's return, but in *Ulysses* history blends with myth. In fact, Parnell is even woven into the same pattern as Odysseus, since the cabman says he will return after "twenty odd years" (*U* 649.14).[19]

Applying this insight to history, Joyce could have taken character after character and brought them alive again by spinning them through Odysseus' formula for heroic action: escape, exile, and finally return after overcoming countless barriers. Try, for instance, two of Joyce's favorite heroes who loom behind the world of *Ulysses*—Henrik Ibsen and Giordano Bruno. Ibsen, like Joyce, had difficulty achieving recognition for his genius in his native land. Disgruntled, he left for the Continent and settled in Italy, where, self-exiled in Rome, he wrote his best plays about his homeland. He finally gained the recognition he deserved, but success only came after he sacrificed happiness in Norway in order faithfully to pursue his art abroad.

Similarly, Bruno, the Renaissance writer and philosopher, was

19. Gifford and Seidman, *Notes for Joyce*, 452, point out that Bloom must have been aware that Parnell had been dead for thirteen years. But they fail to recognize how Joyce consciously fits all these stories of return into a twenty-year pattern.

forced by the Church to flee his native Italy because of his heretical views. Wandering from foreign court to foreign court, Bruno steadfastly stuck to his quest for the truth. Finally, longing to return to Italy, he hoped that his philosophy could be reconciled with the teachings of the Church. But, upon returning, he was betrayed to the authorities by a friend and given the choice of renouncing his views or being burned as a heretic. Refusing to recant, he, like the saint from whom Stephen derives his name, became a martyr for his vision of the truth.

Furthermore, the *Odyssey*, comprehensive itself, gives birth to one of the most comprehensive traditions in Western literature. As he immersed himself deeper and deeper in the Odyssean tradition Joyce must have felt that it continually suggested or justified his enterprise in *Ulysses*. The mighty Dante and Shakespeare had prepared the way for giving Odysseus new speeches and character traits. Gerhart Hauptmann, Joyce's favorite modern dramatist after Ibsen, wrote *A Bow for Odysseus* (1914), in which he confines the action to one day and questions Penelope's fidelity.[20] Samuel Butler anticipates Stephen's theory about authors hiding themselves within their texts by claiming that the *Odyssey* was written by a young girl who appears in the poem as Nausicaa. In fact Joyce could do without Butler's transformation of the author's sex; he could point directly to the hidden authorial figure, Demodocus, the blind poet who entertains at the Phaeacian's banquet for Odysseus by singing, Homer-like, of the Trojan War.

Because he could not read Greek, Joyce was forced to rely on even another aspect of the *Odyssey* tradition: that of translation. The two translators most important for Joyce were Samuel Butler, who treats the story as a naturalistic novel, and Charles Lamb, who admits that he sacrificed "manners to passion" in order to "make [the story] more attractive and give it more the air of romance."[21] Joyce could be said to have combined their two methods within *Ulysses*. But more important, the fact that different authors translate the *Odyssey* into

20. See Dougald McMillan, "Influences of Gerhardt [*sic*] Hauptmann in Joyce's *Ulysses*," *James Joyce Quarterly*, IV (Winter, 1967), 107–19.
21. Hugh Kenner, *The Pound Era* (Berkeley: University of California Press, 1971), 48–49; William MacDonald (ed.), *The Works of Charles Lamb* (7 vols.; London: J. M. Dent, 1903), VII, 115.

English, with varying effects, shows that telling the same story with a different style changes the story. Or put another way, ingenious use of language can make an old story new again.

Even more important than joining the honored company of these artists, Joyce has the opportunity to tell the story of his own life in such a way as to fit the heroic Odyssean pattern. Self-exiled from his native Ireland, he wanders from Trieste to Zurich to Paris, writing about Dublin.[22] Not daring to risk return because, among other reasons, he could be threatened by libel from a pack of betrayers seeking revenge against the forger of their conscience for his published version of the truth, Joyce remains a wandering exile in Europe. But although exiled in life, in art he accomplishes his return through the writing of *Ulysses*. Unable to make a return through space (*nebeneinander*) and time (*nacheinander*) to the world of Dublin he once knew, Joyce creates a parallel world of the imagination that he, lord and giver of life, can manipulate and control. To his self-created Dublin the creator returns, like Shakespeare's ghost, crying out to those who might have forgotten, "Remember me."

Conveniently, the twenty years' absence of Odysseus, Shakespeare, Parnell, Ben Bolt, Rip van Winkle, and Caoc O'Leary corresponds to the twenty years between Joyce's original departure for Paris and the publishing of *Ulysses*. Similarly his "seven years' sentence" (*JJ* 533) during which he wrote *Ulysses* corresponds to the seven years D. B. Murphy spent sailing about away from his wife. In fact, at the time that he was writing the "Eumaeus" chapter, Joyce acknowledged the personal significance of the numbers seven and twenty. On 24 November 1920 he wrote to John Quinn: "I began *Ulysses* in 1914 and shall finish it, I suppose, in 1921. This is, I think, the twentieth address at which I have written it—and the coldest" (*Letters, III* 30).

Thus, Joyce finds that his address, like Murphy's, continually changes during the seven years it takes to write his *Odyssey*. Also like Murphy, who may really be A. Boudin, Joyce's name continually changes in the story he narrates. At times this author, who is all in all, has characteris-

22. Michael Seidel, *Epic Geography: James Joyce's "Ulysses"* (Princeton: Princeton University Press, 1976), 89, points out that Joyce's own odyssey along a northwest axis repeats that of Odysseus.

tics of Stephen Dedalus; at other times, of Leopold Bloom; at others, of Murphy himself. His name and address are like an algebraic unknown, continually changing value, causing some difficulties with self-identity. As we are told in "Eumaeus," "For as to who he in reality was let XX equal my right name and address, as Mr Algebra remarks *passim*" (*U* 658.17). The XX, which as a roman numeral equals twenty, reminds us of the personal importance of twenty for Joyce, which is another reason for having *Ulysses* last about twenty hours.

Ulysses, then, becomes Joyce's personal odyssey for autobiographical as well as aesthetic reasons. On the one hand, the book consists of and alludes to experiences from Joyce's own life. On the other, in writing the book he arranges and orders his life in such a way as to make it correspond to the *Odyssey*. Joyce turns himself into the hero of his book by writing the book of himself according to the proper script. It is no accident that he shares the title page with his childhood hero and his artistic father. Ultimately, Joyce's aesthetic odyssey and his autobiographical odyssey merge in the writing of *Ulysses*. His aesthetic is autobiographical and his autobiography a work of art. The result is that the fictional autobiography Joyce forges for himself holds more currency than factual biographies about his life, because "when all was said and done, the lies a fellow told about himself couldn't probably hold a proverbial candle to the wholesale whoppers other fellows coined about him" (*U* 636.18–21). By weaving and unweaving his image within his work of art, Joyce, like Stephen's Shakespeare, accounts for his perspective as a component part of its reality.

Part II

A Language So Encyclopaedic

Chapter Three

Done Half by Design

So in this book of "many happy returns" (*U* 93.12–13), first published on Joyce's birthday, it is Joyce who leads the stampede of homeward-bound heroes. *Ulysses* seems the perfect example of a novel-epic written by an author in complete control of language. It is Joyce who exhibits power over his creation by making extremes meet in "jewgreek is greekjew" (*U* 504.12). It is Joyce who, through the act of writing, verbally merges Stephen and Bloom into Stoom and Blephen (*U* 682.27, 29). It is Joyce who forges the book into a circular return story pattern ("curves the world admires" [*U* 176.26]), and in view of the book's countless events and details, such forgery is a heroic act in itself. As we hear in "Eumaeus": "High educational abilities though he possessed, he experienced no little difficulty in making both ends meet" (*U* 621.21–22).

In emphasizing the power Joyce exhibits in forging the events of his story to conform to the Odyssean return story pattern, I take issue with an entire strain of *Ulysses* criticism that, tired perhaps of the search for trivial connections set in motion by the Stuart Gilbert approach to *Ulysses*, minimizes the importance of the *Odyssey* in Joyce's structuring of his book. In the widely praised collection of essays *James Joyce's "Ulysses,"* editors Clive Hart and David Hayman write, "Certain assumptions were shared at least tacitly by all of our contributors. First, the parallel with the *Odyssey* is not only present but

85

ironic. It is, however, not responsible for the form taken by the book, whatever its role in the shaping of episodes and actions and in the choice of styles." On the contrary, I contend that the return story pattern of the *Odyssey* does help shape the form taken by the book. Joyce's use of the *Odyssey* is not merely a mechanical scaffolding as Pound thought, nor is it merely there to act as a continual comparison between past and present as Eliot thought. Instead it is one of the most important structural elements of the book. Michael Seidel has recently shown how carefully Joyce used Victor Bérard's maps of Odysseus' voyage to structure the movement of characters through the streets of Dublin.[1] Furthermore, the book's circular structure is well known. It starts with an S and ends with an S, starts with the techniques of narrative, catechism, and monologue and ends with them repeated in order in the *Nostos*. Like the world, the book has "no ends really because it's round" (*U* 378.30–31). More important, the *Odyssey* gives Joyce a pattern and a metaphor by which he can unify the events of the tale of the telling and the naturalistic tale. While Bloom completes his personal odyssey in the naturalistic tale, Joyce in the tale of the telling traces his own heroic odyssey, which he completes by writing *Ulysses*. Finally, the reader himself must become Odysseus if he is successfully to steer his way through the pages of the book.

For Joyce, the pattern more than the epiphany or the symbol is a major structural device. In emphasizing the pattern, Joyce participated in and helped initiate a major twentieth-century insight. This is how Hugh Kenner puts it: "Men came to understand early in the 20th Century, all realities whatever are patterned energies. If mass is energy (Einstein) then all matter exemplifies knottings, the self-interference inhibiting radiant expansion at the speed of light. Like a slip-knot, a radioactive substance expends itself. Elsewhere patterns weave, unweave, reweave: light becomes leaf becomes coal becomes light."[2] It is no accident that Kenner models his last phrase on Stephen's sentence, "God becomes man becomes fish becomes barnacle goose becomes featherbed mountain" (*U* 50.13–14). In *Ulysses*, Joyce continually

1. Clive Hart and David Hayman (eds.), *James Joyce's "Ulysses"* (Berkeley: University of California Press, 1974), viii; Michael Seidel, *Epic Geography: James Joyce's "Ulysses"* (Princeton: Princeton University Press, 1976).

2. Hugh Kenner, *The Pound Era* (Berkeley: University of California Press, 1971), 153.

weaves, unweaves, and reweaves the return story pattern. On one hand, he reduces it to its essential elements; on the other, he shows the pattern's infinite variety by repeating and elaborating it *ad infinitum*. By showing the uniqueness of each individual, Joyce shows the sameness of all experience.

Joyce's use of the pattern does not start with *Ulysses*. I would like to turn to his use of the pattern in earlier works, in order to see what implications structuring an entire work by a pattern carries for the individual characters in the naturalistic tale, before I return to its implications for Joyce's act of writing.

As early as 1900, in the essay "Drama and Life," Joyce was concerned with realities existing as patterned energies. He creates the two categories of drama and literature. Drama concerns itself with underlying laws, the universal; literature, with the individual agents who carry out these laws, the particular.

Human society is the embodiment of changeless laws which the whimsicalities and circumstances of men and women involve and overwrap. The realm of literature is the realm of these accidental manners and humours—a spacious realm; and the true literary artist concerns himself mainly with them. Drama has to do with the underlying laws first, in all their nakedness and divine serenity, and only secondarily with the motley agents who bear them out. . . . By drama I understand the interplay of passions to portray truth; drama is strife, evolution, movement in whatever way unfolded; it exists before it takes form, independently; it is conditioned but not controlled by its scene. (*CW* 40–41)

Joyce then asks whether drama and literature can be joined. "Shall we put life—real life—on stage?" His answer deserves lengthy quotation.

Still I think out of the dreary sameness of existence, a measure of dramatic life may be drawn. Even the most commonplace, the deadest among the living, may play a part in a great drama. It is a sinful foolishness to sigh back for the good old times, to feed the hunger of us with the cold stones they afford. Life we must accept as we see it before our eyes, men and women as we meet them in the real world, not as we apprehend them in the world of faery. The great human comedy in which each has share, gives limitless scope to the true artist, today as yesterday and as in years gone. The forms of things, as the earth's crust, are changed. The timbers of the ships of Tarshish are falling asunder or eaten by the wanton sea; time has broken into the fastnesses of the mighty; the gardens of Armida are become as treeless wilds. But the deathless passions, the human verities which so found expression then, are indeed deathless, in the heroic cycle, or in the scientific age, *Lohengrin*, the drama of which unfolds itself in a scene of seclusion, amid half-lights, is not an Antwerp legend but a world drama. *Ghosts*, the action of which passes in a common parlour, is of universal import. (*CW* 45)

For Joyce, the individual and the universal, drama and literature can and must be combined. In 1900 the question remained, How?

If the epiphanies and classical temper of *Stephen Hero* were not enough, by the time of *Dubliners* Joyce was starting to learn how to become the priest of the imagination who could imbue the daily bread of existence with a spiritual component without seeming to change its outward appearance. He does so by forging together individual stories into a larger pattern.

Dubliners sketches the case history of characters whose lives are predetermined by a Dublin pattern of life, a basic pattern with infinite variations. Although the Dubliners make apparently varying choices, they cannot escape the closed circle that this pattern describes. The fate of the Dubliners is to start in Dublin, to try to escape, and to end where they began. In trying to escape, they become entangled in a narrow world of self-deception and turn into that which they flee. Those who marry find themselves no less alone than those who do not. Counterpointing Eveline, who passively succumbs to paralysis, Jimmy Doyle tries to escape the dull life of Dublin for a fast Continental one, but he ends, like all Irishmen, losing to an Englishman. Farrington tries to escape the unjust master-slave pecking order of his office and ends unjustly beating his son. Virtually every character dreams of escaping Dublin, but only Ignatius Gallaher has gotten away. Yet Paris and London have done nothing to alter his vulgar manner. He remains a quintessential Dubliner. Even Little Chandler's and Farrington's totally opposite temperaments do not save them from a common fate: boring jobs and unhappy marriages. The only difference comes when Chandler is brought to tears by his child, while Farrington brings tears to his child's eyes. As Hugh Kenner says, "Time, place, personnel alter; the pattern remains."[3]

3. Kenner, *The Pound Era*, 147.

Joyce provides a miniature image of this closed circular action at the end of "The Dead," when Gabriel tells the story of Johnny, the shortsighted horse, who mistook King William's statue for the mill. While describing how Johnny walked in circles around the statue, Gabriel enacts the pattern of action by walking in circles himself. Similarly shortsighted, Dubliners spend their entire lives walking only to return to where they began.

The pattern the Dubliners are doomed to follow is what José Ortega y Gasset calls the pattern of reality as opposed to the pattern of adventure. "Soon after we begin living we become aware of the confines of our prison. It takes us thirty years at the most to recognize the limits within which our possibilities will move. We take stock of reality, which is like measuring the length of the chain which binds our feet. Then we say: 'Is this life? Nothing more than this? A closed cycle which is repeated always identical?' This is a dangerous hour for every man."[4] It is especially dangerous for the Dubliners because they rarely become aware of the exact nature of the confines of their prison. If we scrupulously examine the lives of the Dubliners we realize that, more than being trapped by the routine of Dublin life, they are trapped by their perception of that life.

In *Deceit, Desire and the Novel*, René Girard defines the essential characteristic of Flaubert's characters and, in doing so, aptly describes the characters in *Dubliners*.

We must turn to Jules de Gaultier for the definition of this "bovarysm" which he reveals in almost every one of Flaubert's characters: "The same ignorance, the same inconsistency, the same absence of individual reaction seem to make them fated to obey the suggestion of an external milieu, for lack of an auto-suggestion from within." In his famous essay, entitled "Bovarysm," Gaultier goes on to observe that in order to reach their goal, which is to "see themselves as they are not," Flaubert's heroes find a "model" for themselves and "imitate" from the person they have decided to be, all that can be imitated, everything exterior, appearance, gesture, intonation, and dress.[5]

---

4. José Ortega y Gasset, *Meditations on Quixote*, trans. Evelyn Rugg and Diego Maria (New York: W. W. Norton, 1961), 132.
5. René Girard, *Deceit, Desire and the Novel*, trans. Yvonne Freccero (Baltimore: Johns Hopkins University Press, 1965), 5.

The characters in *Dubliners* descend directly from Flaubert's heroes and heroines. Discontented with themselves, they look outside themselves in an attempt to find happiness. In doing so, they focus upon some external model whom they try to imitate. Many of these models come from fictional literature, whether it be Wild West stories of "true adventure"; a Walter Scott novel with a "real" chivalric hero; cheap melodrama with kind openhearted sailors named Frank; romantic poetry with melancholy but passionate poets of the Celtic school; or a Hauptmann play with an orderly, controlled artist named Michael Kramer. Dubliners even turn people encountered in everyday life into fictional models. Little Chandler turns vulgar journalist Gallaher into a successful writer. Gabriel turns dead Michael Furey into a passionate lover. The tendency to transform people into symbols, rather than accept them as they are, especially afflicts potential lovers. Eveline sees Frank as her savior. Mr. Duffy first idealizes Mrs. Sinico into a sympathetic philosopher and then reduces her to a sex-starved Wife of Bath. Gabriel places Gretta in a sentimental picture entitled *Distant Music*. By allowing a view of the world that originates in fictions external to themselves to dictate their responses to the world, the Dubliners fall victim to those fictions. Even more than the predetermined pattern that they all must live, their own mind-forged manacles paralyze the Dubliners.

A look at *Dubliners* makes it clear that the return story pattern need not lead to the comedy of *Ulysses*. Something has happened to the Dublin pattern of life by the time it reaches *Ulysses* to turn it from a series of frustrated escapes to many happy returns. For one, a new structural pattern in *A Portrait* intervenes.

Stephen Dedalus is an interesting case because he is a Dubliner with a difference, one more aware of the confines of his prison. The pattern that Stephen traces is not a circular one but a transcendent one, one that tries to fly from Dublin's labyrinth, a labyrinth whose symmetry in *Ulysses* is associated with death. "Always find out this equal to that, symmetry under a cemetery wall" (*U* 278.19–20). "Cemetery put in of course on account of the symmetry" (*U* 121.16–17). The soaring pattern that tries to transcend the circularity of everyday life has its own literary tradition. It was especially popular in nineteenth-century works that helped shape Stephen's mind. As Michael Seidel points out, Stephen's thoughts abound with patterns of *Verstiegenheit*, often borrowed from nineteenth-century works: Goethe's "Walpurgisnacht" in *Faust*, Blake's *Milton*, Shelley's *Prometheus Unbound*, Flaubert's *La Tentation de Saint Antoine*, Ibsen's *Peer Gynt*.[6] Seidel might have mentioned even more of Stephen's heroes who justify his pattern of endless wandering and exile. There is Columbanus, the early "priest of the eternal imagination" who left Ireland in order to spread religion to the Continent, never to return again. There is Oscar Wilde, another exiled Dublin artist, from whom Stephen borrows quotations and *fin de siècle* poetic style.

As Hugh Kenner first noticed, the book that Stephen dominates is structured by the rising and falling pattern of his heroes. At the end of each chapter Stephen soars to a victorious climax, only to be forced to return to earth early in the next chapter.[7] Joyce outlines the essential elements of this pattern in the first page and a half of the book. The remainder of the action continually elaborates this rising and falling action, gaining complexity with variations along the way. One of these elaborations, important for Joyce's technique in *Ulysses*, is the introduction of a mythical correspondence—the Daedalus myth—to serve as an archetypal pattern for the book's structure.

Looked at from one point of view, the pattern of *A Portrait* approaches the circular pattern of *Dubliners*. Stephen's flights of the imagination are compelled by the force of gravity (32 ft/sec^2) to return to earth. Stephen himself is called back from Paris at his mother's death to visit a cemetery in Dublin. But Icarus' flight does not end in a completed orbit. His flight is discontinuous and dead-ends in the sea. The attempt to transcend the inevitable circularity of life can lead to the fate of Icarus. Small wonder that, in *Ulysses*, Stephen has a fear of water.

In this respect Bloom seems closer to the Dubliners than does Stephen. He shares the Dubliners' circular pattern of life. While Stephen's first important act in *Ulysses* is to leave his temporary dwelling

6. Seidel, *Epic Geography*, 84.
7. Hugh Kenner, "The *Portrait* in Perspective," in Seon Givens (ed.), *James Joyce: Two Decades of Criticism* (New York: Vanguard Press, 1948), 132–74.

place, vowing not to return (he ends the book still wandering), Bloom leaves 7 Eccles Street only to return. Also like the Dubliners, he fantasizes; he gets facts wrong; he tries to hide himself from the fact of Molly's adultery. He cannot transcend the limitations of seeing from his personal point of view and of creating fictions about the world. Nor can he avoid playing roles that are received and suggested from outside himself. In short, he is a close relative to the bovaryan character; his behavior and the bovaryan character's are not mutually exclusive. But, ultimately, a qualitative difference exists between the two. It has to do with the quality of Bloom's perception of the world.

Bloom accepts his limited perspective. This keeps his perception of the world open; he allows evidence from the perceived to contradict the meaning he forces upon it. The quality of Bloom's perception changes the quality of his life. Caught in the same circular pattern as other Dubliners, Bloom transforms this pattern into a source of fulfillment. Arnold Goldman (via Kierkegaard) pinpoints Bloom's unique power of perception. "In the sphere of nature repetition exists in its immovable necessity. In the sphere of spirit the problem is not to contrive to get change out of repetition and find oneself comfortable under it . . . but the problem is to transform repetition into something inward, into the proper task of freedom."[8] Bloom becomes Joyce's hero because, ironically, he does not seek heroism in impossible quests or false models. Stephen unsuccessfully tries to escape Dublin's labyrinth by emulating Hamlet, Shakespeare, Lucifer, and countless others, but Bloom merely plays himself and unconsciously takes on characteristics of the hero Odysseus, who completes a circular pattern of fulfillment, not frustration.

Joyce's power as a writer, like Bloom's as a character, has to do with his ability to transform repetition, since in writing *Ulysses* he is self-consciously returning to the works of two of the most important writers in the West: Homer and Shakespeare. Not accidentally both of these writers structure their works by the return story pattern, a pattern repeated and transformed by Joyce. Thus, it is not surpris-

8. Arnold Goldman, *The Joyce Paradox* (Evanston: Northwestern University Press, 1968), 156–57.

ing to hear Lenehan remark after telling M'Coy the story of Bloom repeating the act of identifying already identified constellations in the sky, "There's a touch of the artist about old Bloom" (*U* 235.17).

The similarity between Bloom's artistic touch and Joyce's deserves closer scrutiny. Despite the fact that we do not get to read the sketch Bloom might manage about him and Molly or his proposed *My Experiences in a Cabman's Shelter*, three of his completed works are listed in "Ithaca." A close reading of them reveals remarkable similarities with Joyce's techniques in *Ulysses*.[9] Few pieces of literature have a more convoluted subject matter than Bloom's first poem, a poem about the author's desire to see his poem in print.

> *An ambition to squint*
> *At my verses in print*
> *Makes me hope that for these you'll find room.*
> *If you so condescend*
> *Then please place at the end*
> *The name of yours truly, L. Bloom.* (*U* 678.3—8)

In his next two pieces, Bloom adopts the technique of hiding his own name within his handiwork. His second work of art is a collection of anagrams formed by rearranging the letters of Leopold Bloom (*U* 678.13—17). Finally, in the poem sent to Molly on 14 February 1888, we discover that the first letters of each line spell POLDY (*U* 678.21—25). Bloom, like Shakespeare and Joyce, leaves an image of himself behind in his works of art.

To note more of Bloom's artistic qualities, we will have to return to Stephen's Shakespeare theory. Bloom shares a number of qualities with the portrait of the artist presented by Stephen in the library. Stephen declares that the artist, capable of creating a world out of himself, is an androgynous angel. Bloom himself has a number of androgynous characteristics (see *JJ* 477). While Bloom's feminine side surfaces most prominently in the famous transexual scene in "Circe," Joyce works throughout to give Bloom characteristics of "the new womanly

9. See a very different discussion of Bloom's writings in James H. Maddox, *Joyce's "Ulysses" and the Assault upon Character* (New Brunswick: Rutgers University Press, 1978), 180—81.

man" (*U* 493.30). His middle name is Paula. He has a "masculine feminine passive active hand" (*U* 674.34). Even his abandoned name, Virag, connotes virago, a mannish woman. As a boy he played a female in the school version of *Vice Versa*. Finally, in the library Stephen claims that "Boccaccio's Calandrino was the first and last man who felt himself with child" (*U* 207.18–20), but in "Circe," Bloom *"bears eight male yellow and white children"* (*U* 494.24–25).

Furthermore, while Bloom's repetition of the return story pattern of the *Odyssey* is familiar to most readers, his repetition of the return story pattern Stephen constructs for Shakespeare is not so widely acknowledged. Yet the pattern is familiar. Bloom leaves 7 Eccles Street to try to escape the fact that his Penelope / Ann is about to cuckold him. After wandering the streets of Dublin, Bloom returns home and revenges his cuckoldry in his mind-created fictions. While wandering away from home, Bloom, like Shakespeare, indulges in thoughts, if not acts, of scortatory love. Although appearing shocked by the medical students' talk of birth control in "Oxen of the Sun," Bloom carries a french letter in his wallet (*U* 370.39, *U* 772.33), perhaps a reminder that in "Scylla and Charybdis" the artist George Moore is said to be a "lecturer on French letters" (*U* 214.41). Further, Zarathustra is also described as the "sometime regius professor of French letters to the university of Oxtail" (*U* 393.20–21).

More particularly, Bloom fits Stephen's portrait of the artist because the first time that he sees Blazes he adopts an air of detachment by looking at his well-pared nails. "Mr Bloom reviewed the nails of his left hand, then those of his right hand. The nails, yes. Is there anything more in him that they she sees? Fascination. Worst man in Dublin. That keeps him alive. They sometimes feel what a person is. Instinct. But a type like that. My nails. I am just looking at them: well pared. And after: thinking alone" (*U* 92.23–28). Joyce's other famous nail-parer is Stephen's godlike artist of *A Portrait* who also expresses his detachment and indifference by adopting this pose. Furthermore, in *A Portrait* and elsewhere in Joyce's work, nail-paring suggests masturbation or latent homosexuality. Tusker Boyle, a principal in the "smugging" incident, is called "Lady Boyle because he was always at his nails, paring them" (*P* 42). This helps explain why Mr. Gleeson, who also has long pointed nails ("perhaps he pared them too like Lady Boyle" [*P* 45]), lets the boys off without flogging them hard. In fact the entire smugging incident is interspersed in Stephen's mind with the time that Eileen (who "had long thin cool white hands too because she was a girl" [*P* 42]) puts her hand in Stephen's pocket and runs away laughing. What she feels in Stephen's pocket other than his hand to make her laugh we are not told, but we can imagine. We are, in fact, told, "By thinking of things you could understand them" (*P* 43).

With these images in mind, we can see how Joyce uses Bloom's detached look at his nails when confronted with Blazes to repeat Shakespeare's escape behind the indifferent pose of the invisible dramatic artist when confronted with his possible cuckoldry. And the parallel continues. Just as Shakespeare hides himself from himself in the world of art, so the next time that Bloom sees Blazes (who, according to Molly, "has no manners nor no refinement" [*U* 776.20–21] and who writes with a "bold hand" [*U* 61.37)[10] he escapes into an art museum. Later, confronted with Blazes in "Sirens," "I feel so lonely Bloom" continues to try and refine himself out of existence; he would rather "see, not be seen" (*U* 265.17). Appropriately, when the cuckolded image of Shakespeare appears in "Circe," he says to Bloom "*in dignified ventriloquy,*" "Thou thoughtest as how thou wastest invisible. Gaze" (*U* 567.22, 23–24). While the actual adultery takes place, Bloom turns to yet another discipline of art as a vehicle of escape. This time he uses the music in the hotel to block out the music that Blazes and Molly are making at 7 Eccles Street. "Wish they'd sing more. Keep my mind off" (*U* 280.34–35). Unwittingly, however, Bloom makes a comment on the musical performance that turns the reader's mind back to Blazes and Molly. "Wonder who's playing. Nice touch" (*U* 270.39–40).

Touch, it turns out, is a word within *Ulysses* that takes on sexual connotations. In "Calypso," Bloom remembers the day Rudy was conceived. Watching two dogs mate, Molly had cried, "Give us a touch, Poldy. God, I'm dying for it" (*U* 89.10–11). This, thinks Bloom, is "how

10. Fritz Senn, "Ex unque Leopold," *English Studies*, XLVIII (December, 1967), 537–43, first makes this connection.

life begins." But, now, lacking the ability to provide Molly with the "touch" she desires, Bloom turns to a masturbatory touch—"the touch of a deadhand cures" (*U* 514.22–23). As Stephen's Shakespeare theory insists, the "touch of the artist" is influenced by his sexual touching. Thus, just as Shakespeare, away from Stratford, turns to writing to create imaginary worlds that compensate for his domestic situation, so Bloom turns to writing and composes a letter to continue his imaginary affair with Martha Clifford.

The comments and actions surrounding Bloom's composition of his letter serve equally well as comments on Joyce's composition of *Ulysses*.[11] For instance, complaints about and difficulties with Joyce's stylistic play in "Sirens" are anticipated by Bloom's remarks on the chapter's background music. "Instance he's playing now. Improvising. Might be what you like till you hear the words. Want to listen sharp. Hard. Begin all right: then hear chords a. bit off: feel lost a bit" (*U* 278.25–27). Bloom also reminds us that as Joyce wrote he continually needed to put in his Greek allusions. "Remember write Greek ees" (*U* 279.11). Furthermore, Bloom adopts an air of detachment as he writes. Pretending that he is merely writing an advertisement, he taps his writing pad with a look of boredom. Despite a writer's detached pose, he cannot keep his hidden hand totally refined out of existence. Thus, Bloom is "reflecting fingers on flat pad Pat brought" (*U* 279.16). As Joyce must have occasionally done, Bloom also wonders if it is a folly that he is writing. But then Bloom realizes the motivation for writing. He realizes that husbands have no need to write because they are in physical proximity to the object of their love. We write letters only when we are separated from those to whom we write. Bloom writes "because I'm away from" (*U* 279.28). Similarly, Joyce writes about Dublin because he is away. Writing, motivated by absence rather than by presence, becomes a way of accomplishing a return. Complying with Martha's request, Bloom will send his letters "*by return*" (*U* 78.10, Martha's emphasis). Bloom himself had even tried out Joyce's

11. See Colin MacCabe, *James Joyce and the Revolution of the Word* (London: Macmillan, 1978), 83. "The 'Sirens' can be read as the dramatization of the materiality of language and it is Bloom as the writer in the drama who acts for the reader as the decomposer of the voice and music into material sounds."

technique of having a hero of the past return to walk the streets of present-day Dublin. The title of his uncompleted song is *If Brian Boru could but come back and see old Dublin now* (U 678.28–29).

Art, especially the art of writing, seems to have the power to turn absence into presence, sundering into reconciliation, escape into return. Through his forgery the writer can transform the repetition of daily life and weave it into a comic pattern of many happy returns. Thus, the artist's return story pattern traced by Shakespeare (and Joyce) seems like the *Odyssey*, to lead to a successfully completed homecoming. The successful return is made possible by recognizing, as do Bloom, Odysseus, Shakespeare, and Joyce, individual limitations. For the artist, that especially means abandoning a godlike position outside his work for a return within it, to try no longer to transcend the world but to be part of it, to present neither an objective nor a subjective view of the world but of subjectivity in the world, just as Bloom differentiates his perception of the world from the Dubliners' by admitting his limited point of view and possibility of error as part of it.

But such a harmonious resolution is not exactly the lesson that either Stephen's Shakespeare theory or *Ulysses* offers. While in the late plays Shakespeare achieves reconciliation in art, he does not do so in life. "He passes on towards eternity in undiminished personality, untaught by the wisdom he has written or by the laws he has revealed" (U 197.10–12). When Shakespeare returns to Stratford he does not achieve a reconciliation with Ann. He leaves her his second-best bed. Shakespeare's life traces a return story pattern significantly different from the one recorded in his plays and in the *Odyssey*. Shakespeare's Penelope / Ann does not remain faithful; his son dies, rather than recognize him; there is no celebration of reunion in Stratford. Shakespeare himself returns to Stratford to die.

In *Ulysses*, Bloom faces a situation similar to Shakespeare's. To be sure, he does not arrive home to die, but neither does he achieve a happy reunion. Late in the chapter "Ithaca," Bloom prepares for sleep, his mind wandering to thoughts of travel and return:

Would the departed never nowhere nohow reappear?
Ever he would wander, selfcompelled, to the extreme limit of his com-

etary orbit, beyond the fixed stars and variable suns and telescopic planets, astronomical waifs and strays, to the extreme boundary of space, passing from land to land, among peoples, amid events. Somewhere imperceptibly he would hear and somehow reluctantly, suncompelled, obey the summons of recall. Whence, disappearing from the constellation of the Northern Crown he would somehow reappear reborn above delta in the constellation of Cassiopeia and after incalculable eons of peregrination return an estranged avenger, a wreaker of justice on malefactors, a dark crusader, a sleeper awakened, with financial resources (by supposition) surpassing those of Rothschild or of the silver king. (*U* 727.35–728.10)

Here is the familiar return story pattern, with allusions to many of its most famous heroes: estranged avengers (Odysseus, the Count of Monte Cristo, Stephen's Shakespeare) and sleepers awakened (Rip van Winkle, Hamlet's ghost, Odysseus at Ithaca). But all these heroes are fictional. Bloom can achieve a successfully completed heroic odyssey only in the world of his imagination, an imagination conditioned by the fictions of his culture.

In the world of Dublin, 16 June 1904, Bloom's return is not possible because of the limits of space and time.

What would render such return irrational?
An unsatisfactory equation between an exodus and return in time through reversible space and an exodus and return in space through irreversible time. (*U* 728.11–14)

Successfully completed odysseys occur more often in works of fiction than in life. The circle does not close perfectly. It does not, because we live in a world of time. In a world of time, there can be no perfect repetition as when two points coincide in space. The myth of the successful return depends on the myth of spatialized time. But, as Bloom knows, the irreversibility of time renders a perfect return impossible. At the end of "Nausicaa" he thinks, "The year returns. History repeats itself" (*U* 377.1) but he soon adds, "No. Returning not the same" (*U* 377.13). Then, as the *Nostos* begins in "Eumaeus," he warns, "And the coming back was the worst thing you ever did because it went without saying you would feel out of place as things always moved with the times" (*U* 651.40–42).

Of all the returning heroes alluded to in "Eumaeus" very few really achieve successful returns. Rip van Winkle, Ben Bolt, Enoch Arden, and Caoc O'Leary all return to changed worlds. Moses dies before reaching the promised land. Parnell is brought down by his Judas-like friends and the Church. Even Odysseus is attacked by a pack of dogs and a horde of suitors. Bloom again: "Still, as regards return, you were a lucky dog if they didn't set the terrier at you directly you got back. Then a lot of shillyshally usually followed" (*U* 650.6–9).

But Bloom is a fictional character just as Odysseus is, and Odysseus, despite the hardships he faces, does achieve a successful return. Why doesn't Joyce allow his fictional character the same fate? It is worth looking more closely at the Odyssean myth to speculate on how its pattern differs from that of *Ulysses*. To do so I will draw on the work of the Frenchman Jacques Derrida.

In his most widely read essay translated into English, Derrida speculates on the concept of the center and the importance it has played in Western thought.[12] Derrida claims that the notion of a center is essential for our understanding of structure; we cannot imagine a structure without a center around which to structure itself. While Derrida does not challenge the need for a center—it is a necessary fiction—he does challenge the need to grant a center ontological status. For instance, it is only by fixing a center that time can be spatialized. Like Heidegger before him, Derrida challenges the desire to spatialize time by indulging in the myth of a fixed center. The myth of a fixed center falls prey to what Derrida terms logocentric thought. Along with others, most notably his countryman Jacques Lacan, Derrida links logocentric thought in the West with the belief in the presence of the father. An entire system of social and political order results from Christianity's myth giving authority to the Logos; God the Father; the Word of the Father; and the sacred text embodying his Word. If this sounds surprisingly like Stephen's speculations on fatherhood in the library, it is, I would claim, because Joyce has anticipated the recent demystification of logocentric thought without succumbing to its tendency to adopt a rhetoric of anxiety or crisis. In fact, one of the most

12. Jacques Derrida, "Structure, Sign, and Play," in *The Structuralist Controversy*, ed. Richard Macksey and Eugene Donato (Baltimore: Johns Hopkins University Press, 1972), 247–72.

important differences between the return story patterns of the *Odyssey* and *Ulysses* is that the *Odyssey* affirms the myth of fatherhood as a fixed center, while *Ulysses* questions it.

Perhaps I should quote once more Stephen's oft-quoted remarks on fatherhood.

Fatherhood, in the sense of conscious begetting, is unknown to man. It is a mystical estate, an apostolic succession, from only begetter to only begotten. On that mystery and not on the madonna which the cunning Italian intellect flung to the mob of Europe the church is founded and founded irremovably because founded, like the world, macro- and microcosm upon the void. Upon incertitude, upon unlikelihood. *Amor matris*, subjective and objective genitive, may be the only true thing in life. Paternity may be a legal fiction. Who is the father of any son that any son should love him or he any son? (*U* 207.20–30)

Far from abstract theory, Stephen's doubts about fatherhood are rooted in a basic biological fact: a male can never be certain that he has sired his son or daughter. While a female carries her child within her for nine months and is still connected to it at birth by the umbilical cord, after conception a male is totally cut off from his child. The child no longer needs the father to be born or to exist. In a sense, then, every father adopts his child. While a mother's responsibility and authority are thrust upon her (only by abortion or after birth can she abdicate her responsibility for helping create the child), a father gains authority only when he acknowledges responsibility for his role in creating the child. A father's authority exists as a result of a claim. In a patriarchal society, that claim is made through a linguistic act: giving the child the father's name. As a result of the father's claim to responsibility through the act of naming, a child becomes legitimate. But because a father has no connection to his child at birth, because his presence is not even necessary, a male's claim to the authority of fatherhood is always subject to doubt; the child's legitimacy may be a counterfeit legitimacy, the father's authority a counterfeit authority.

Belief in the continuity from father to child recorded in the child's name is possible only through faith in the mother's fidelity. When that faith is disrupted, doubt takes over. During the hour that Molly is being mounted by Blazes, Bloom remembers a comment by Simon Dedalus in "Hades": "Wise child that knows her father, Dedalus said. Me?" (*U* 273.8)—an echo, with a difference, of both Telemachus in the *Odyssey*, "Mother tells me that I am his son, but I know not, for no one knows his own father" (*Odyssey* I. 215), and Launcelot in *The Merchant of Venice*, "It is a wise father that knows his own child" (II.ii.70–71). Unlike a matriarchy, in a patriarchy continuity from generation to generation, founded as it is on a possibly legal fiction, is always subject to doubt.

It is interesting that, faced with the dilemma of uncertain paternity, the theologian Gabriel Marcel distinguishes between true fatherhood and mere procreation, by relying on aesthetic vocabulary. According to Marcel, procreation for a male is merely a gesture that "can be performed in almost total unconsciousness and which, at least in extreme cases, is nothing but a letting go, an emptying of something which is over-full." Fatherhood, on the other hand, involves a "creative vow"; that is, a conscious act that acknowledges and carries out responsibility for what one has helped create.[13] But because of the uncertainty of paternity, this creative vow is no proof of authentic fatherhood. The claim could as easily be made by an imposter. The name giver may be a counterfeiter. If the father's claim to authority over his child is exposed as a legal fiction, then the successful completion of an odyssey returning father to family becomes problematic.

Looked at in this way, the return story pattern of the *Odyssey* takes on even more importance, for it is the successful completion of Odysseus' return to home and family that helps create the myth holding the patriarchal family together. Perhaps the most mythical element in the *Odyssey* is not Odysseus' heroic adventures but Penelope's twenty years of fidelity. Her fidelity is of the utmost importance: without it Odysseus' return would be meaningless. Her fidelity, combined with Odysseus' acknowledgment of his responsibility to return home, holds the family together. The components of the myths that unite their domestic family deserve closer scrutiny.

First, we see that the family is structured around the immovable bed at the center of the domestic circle. Second, the family holds together despite the father's absence of twenty years. In fact, as Telemachus makes clear, he does not even know his own father. Third, Odysseus does return, although unrecognized. That is not quite true.

13. Gabriel Marcel, "The Creative Vow as the Essence of Fatherhood," in his *Homo Viator*, trans. Emma Craufurd (London: Camelot Press, 1951), 98–124.

Argos, his dog, recognizes him, and later his maid recognizes a scar inscribed on his skin, but his own son does not. Remember, "no one knows his own father."

Yet because of Penelope's unquestionable fidelity, the family can reunite, Odysseus can once again sleep in the immovable bed at the center of the domestic structure, and Telemachus can finally know and recognize his father. The father's presence is felt in spite of his absence. The epic return is successfully achieved because of belief and fidelity. Penelope's belief that Odysseus will return allows her to remain faithful; Odysseus' belief in Penelope's fidelity spurs him to return; Telemachus' belief in his parents allows him to accept as his father a man he does not even recognize. Here, then, is the foundation of any patriarchal system; faith, a female's fidelity, and a male's acknowledgment of responsibility.

In terms of family roles, the differences between the *Odyssey* and Joyce's rewriting of it in *Ulysses* are major. Rather than a world in which the father returns as a presence to acknowledge his responsibility, *Ulysses* offers a world of impotent, dead, or absent fathers.[14] This fatherless world is mirrored in "Wandering Rocks," the chapter giving a miniature picture of the Dublin scene. Framed by the impotent father figures of Church and State, the chapter records a multitude of failed fathers. Carrying his pound and a half of pork-steaks, Master Dignam thinks of his father. "Never see him again. Death, that is. Pa is dead. My father is dead" (*U* 251.37–38). Paddy Dignam, who consumed too many spirits, can return only as a spirit—a ghost in "Circe." Another victim of Dublin's spirits, Simon Dedalus, has also lost his authority as a father. To his daughter Dilly he says, "Wouldn't care if I was stretched out stiff. He's dead. The man upstairs is dead" (*U* 238.16–17). Later, Simon meets Father Cowley, who has been forced to barricade his dwelling place because of unpaid debts. Meanwhile, the conscript fathers are deliberating on a dead language: "damned Irish language, of our forefathers" (*U* 247.22–23). In the next section, the presence of John Howard Parnell, who looks "ghostbright" (*U* 248.25) at his foe in chess, reminds us of the absence of his brother,

14. See Edmund Epstein, "Stephen's Dance," in his *The Ordeal of Stephen Dedalus* (Carbondale: Southern Illinois University Press, 1971), 156–73, for a list of failed fathers.

the mythical father of Irish politics. Haines adds his bit to the theme of fatherhood by telling Mulligan how he had tackled Stephen that morning on the question of belief in a personal God.

Malachi Mulligan himself has been cited by Simon Dedalus as the person responsible for leading his son Stephen astray. Mulligan's role separating father and son becomes ironic if we remember the words of Malachi 4:5–6: "Behold, I will send you Elijah the prophet before the coming of the great and dreadful day of the Lord: / And he shall turn the heart of the fathers to the children, and the heart of the children to their fathers, lest I come and smite the earth with a curse." Indeed at the end of Mulligan's section the throwaway announcing the coming of Elijah is reported sailing into the Dublin harbor. Perhaps it is also significant that the first appearance of the Elijah throwaway in "Wandering Rocks" occurs directly after Boody Dedalus announces, "Our father who art not in heaven" (*U* 227.3), and that the only other appearance of the throwaway in the chapter comes in Mr. Kernan's section soon after we are given a glimpse of father Simon Dedalus and Father Cowley exchanging greetings.

In fact, Mr. Kernan himself calls attention to the fatherhood theme when he remembers a line from "The Croppy Boy." The events of "The Croppy Boy" warn us that Elijah's attempt to reconcile father and son will not be easy. In "The Croppy Boy," as in *Hamlet*, the son's effort to remain faithful to his departed father leads to increased difficulties. Once the father is dead or rejected, the son does not know which father figure to trust. After his father falls at the siege of Ross, the Croppy Boy is betrayed by paternal representatives of Church and State. On his way to avenge his father's death, the hero kneels in confession and admits that he loves his country more than his king. The priest, however, is a counterfeit priest, who under his robes reveals the scarlet uniform of England. Betrayed by one "father" while trying to remain faithful to another, the Croppy Boy must die. In such a world, it is small wonder that Bloom dreams of being a mother rather than a father, "O, I so want to be a mother" (*U* 494.20).

Other family members do not fare much better. In *Ulysses* few sons are as faithful to their familial fathers as the fictional Croppy Boy or Telemachus. Stephen leaves the house of his father and tries to break paternal ties. He is not alone. Bloom's father had denied the continuity of generations by forsaking the name of his father for the name Bloom. As for wives, Molly cannot remain faithful for twenty hours, not to speak of twenty years. Even the furniture in the Bloom household lacks stability. When Bloom returns home he finds the furniture rearranged. His sore cranium confirms his belief that coming back was hard because "things always moved with the times" (*U* 651.42). Most important, the bed at the center of Bloom's family seems to have been transported all the way from Gibraltar to Dublin. In a world founded on the incertitude of the void rather than the myth of a fixed center, things seem to fall apart. Or, if they do not fall apart, they do not lend themselves to perfect returns.

In "Ithaca," Joyce links the quest for return and the desire for paternity, by having Bloom ponder why his future plans to bring Stephen and Molly together will not work.

What rendered problematic for Bloom the realization of these mutually selfexcluding propositions?

The irreparability of the past: once at a performance of Albert Hengler's circus in the Rotunda, Rutland square, Dublin, an intuitive particoloured clown in quest of paternity had penetrated from the ring to a place in the auditorium where Bloom, solitary, was seated and had publicly declared to an exhilarated audience that he (Bloom) was his (the clown's) papa. The imprevidibility of the future: once in the summer of 1898 he (Bloom) had marked a florin (2s.) with three notches on the milled edge and tendered it in payment of an account due to and received by J. and T. Davy, family grocers, 1 Charlemont Mall, Grand Canal, for circulation on the waters of civic finance, for possible, circuitous or direct, return.

Was the clown Bloom's son?
No.

Had Bloom's coin returned?
Never. (*U* 696.17–34)

Both paternity and return remain unfulfilled.

It takes Paul de Man, writing on circularity in the works of Maurice Blanchot, to give a reason why. The original center, writes de Man, always remains "hidden and out of reach; we are separated from it by the very substance of time. . . . The circularity is not, therefore, a perfect form with which we try to coincide, but a directive that main-

tains and measures the distance that separates us from the center of
things. We can by no means take this circularity for granted: the circle
is a path that we have to construct ourselves and on which we try to
remain. At most, the circularity governs the development of consciousness and is also the guiding principle that shapes the poetic form." In a
temporal world, circularity is inevitable. Yet it is a circularity without a
perfect return. There is always a void that keeps the circle from clos-
ing, no matter how we approach it, and that includes the approach
through art.[15]

So far I have made a distinction between the return story pattern
in life and fiction, claiming that successful returns occur more often in
fiction than in life. Life offers no fixed center around which to structure time; in a work of fiction a writer can impose a center and forge
his work into a successful return story pattern. To a certain extent this
distinction is true, but its assumptions need reexamining. It has been
one of the strengths of so-called deconstructive criticism to stress
that narrative itself is temporal. Thus, when a narrative work, even
one with a finely wrought spatial structure, is read outside the context of its posited center, it inevitably unwinds its spatialization of
time. We can see this unwinding in Joyce's fiction.

Joyce's works have, with good reason, been described as striving
for spatial form.[16] Few novelists have matched Joyce in his ability to
forge his material into a circular structure, making, as I have tried to
show, almost all the book's details conform to the universal return
story pattern. But even in Joyce's works of fiction, beginning and end
do not coincide. When we turn from the last page of *Finnegans Wake*
to the first, the point of view has changed. When the first three techniques of *Ulysses* are repeated in the *Nostos* they are not Narrative
(young), Catechism (personal), and Monologue (male), but Narrative
(old), Catechism (impersonal), and Monologue (female).

15. Paul de Man, "Impersonality in Blanchot," in his *Blindness and Insight* (New York:
Oxford University Press, 1971), 76–77. Martin Heidegger explores as fully as anyone
the link between temporality and circularity that I am suggesting. See especially his
Being and Time, trans. J. Macquarrie and E. Robinson (New York: Harper & Row,
1962), 194–95.
16. Joseph Frank, "Spatial Forms in Modern Literature," in Mark Schorer, Josephine
Miles, and Gordon McKenzie (eds.), *Criticism* (New York: Harcourt, Brace & World,
1958), 379–92.

Worlds of words do not exist in a realm outside time. Made up of language, they are themselves temporal. The circularity that we encounter so persistently in the history of literature could well be a product of language itself, language that, in reaching out to portray a world beyond itself, inevitably turns back naming only itself. In trying to identify, language ends by announcing itself as a sign, leaving a gap between it and what it signifies.

At the end of "Nausicaa," Bloom tries to write a sentence in the sand identifying who he is.

Mr Bloom with his stick gently vexed the thick sand at his foot. Write a message for her. Might remain. What?

I.

Some flatfoot tramp on it in the morning. Useless. Washed away. Tide comes here a pool near her foot. Bend, see my face there, dark mirror, breathe on it, stirs. All these rocks with lines and scars and letters. O, those transparent! Besides they don't know. What is the meaning of that other world. I called you naughty boy because I do not like.

AM. A.

No room. Let it go.

Mr Bloom effaced the letters with his slow boot. Hopeless thing sand. Nothing grows in it. All fades. (*U* 381.29–41)

In "Proteus," Stephen had called the sands of this very beach "language tide and wind have silted here" (*U* 44.36). Although we seek our identity in language, its protean nature makes certain identification impossible.

In this polytropic book, language itself possesses the most turns of all. Joyce is aware, more than most writers, that language can unweave his carefully woven return story pattern, in both the naturalistic tale and the tale of the telling. Joyce is no more successful than Bloom in achieving a presence in the signatures of all things he has left behind for us to read. It is time to turn for a short but closer look at the turning nature of some of the book's language, especially its proper names.

Chapter Four

Names Change: That's All

There is something special about names. A name, according to Ferdinand Saussure, is different from an ordinary noun. Whereas the ordinary nouns *potato* and *soap* signify a concept of "potato" and "soap" as well as referring to something in the world of things, proper names seem to be pure signifiers with only a referent. Furthermore, we tend to grant the connection between a name and its referent a privileged status. A name and an identity become one. It is, for instance, on the basis of names that Stephen constructs his Shakespeare theory (and I my Joyce theory) to prove the return of the artist to his creation. John Eglinton sees Stephen's own name as a force behind his theory. "You make good use of the name, John Eglington allowed. Your own name is strange enough. I suppose it explains your fantastical humour" (*U* 210.31–33).

From the first, Stephen has been made aware of the special qualities of his name. In *A Portrait*, Nasty Roche asks Stephen:

What is your name?
Stephen had answered:
Stephen Dedalus.
Then Nasty Roche had said:
What kind of a name is that? (*P* 8)

Stephen's quest in the book can be seen as an attempt to find the meaning of his name. To do so he must cast off his familial father and fly to his mythical father. In discovering the meaning of his name in a Greek myth, he thinks that he has found his destiny. As Jean Starobinski writes, in an essay on Stendhal's use of names, to which I will refer throughout this chapter: "Our name awaits us. It was there before we knew it, like our body. The common illusion consists in believing that our destiny and our reality are inscribed in it. Thus one confers upon a name the dignity of an essence."[1] In *Ulysses*, Joyce refuses to perpetuate that illusion.

Ulysses also begins by drawing attention to Stephen's name and its disparity with its Dublin setting. "The mockery of it, [Buck] said gaily. Your absurd name, an ancient Greek" (*U* 3.37–38). Dissatisfied with Stephen's given name, Buck gives him one he finds more appropriate, "O, my name for you is the best: Kinch, the knife-blade" (*U* 4.20–21). According to Buck, even the name he bears is artistically motivated. "My name is absurd too: Malachi Mulligan, two dactyls. But it has a Hellenic ring, hasn't it? Tripping and sunny like the buck himself" (*U* 4.4–6).

From the start of *Ulysses* we are asked to pay attention to the act of naming and the seemingly arbitrary way in which names can be acquired. A name might be whimsical or contingent, no more than a label from the outside. A name may have no natural connection with its referent. Indeed, the father, the name giver in a patriarchal society, is cut off from life's cord that connects mother to child. If fatherhood may be a legal fiction, then names obviously are: "Sounds are impostures, Stephen said after a pause of some little time. Like names, Cicero, Podmore, Napoleon, Mr Goodbody, Jesus, Mr Doyle. Shakespeares were as common as Murphies. What's in a name?" (*U* 622.40–43). It is "Eumaeus" more than any chapter in *Ulysses* that warns us to treat all names with suspicion.

In the last chapter I pointed out how few of the heroes listed in "Eumaeus" actually complete successful returns. Their difficulty may not be the result only of the inherent dangers of an odyssey. Their returns may be blocked because they are not the people they represent themselves to be. In the midst of speculation about Parnell's return, Bloom remembers the case of Roger Charles Tichborne, who

1. Jean Starobinski, "Truth in Masquerade," in Victor Brombert (ed.), *Stendhal* (Englewood Cliffs, N.J.: Prentice-Hall, 1962), 115.

had drowned in the shipwreck of the *Bella*. An imposter assumed Tichborne's identity and appeared in London claiming Tichborne's position. With this story Joyce inserts the point that all those claiming to be returning heroes are not to be trusted, nor is a name alone proof of one's identity. Like the figures referred to in the *Odyssey* who came to Ithaca falsely claiming to be Odysseus, or like the false prophets of the Bible, many characters only masquerade as returning heroes and kings. Stephen lists quite a few in "Proteus": "Pretenders: live their lives. The Bruce's brother, Thomas Fitzgerald, silken knight, Perkin Warbeck, York's false scion, in breeches of silk of whiterose ivory, wonder of a day, and Lambert Simnel, with a tail of nans and sutlers, a scullion crowned. All kings' sons. Paradise of pretenders then and now" (*U* 45.25–30).

"Eumaeus" turns out to be *Ulysses*' "paradise of pretenders." Almost every character in the chapter goes under a pseudonym or alias.[2] Skin-the-Goat is rumored to be Fitzharris, the famous invincible. A local jarvey whom he argues with is "obviously bogus" (*U* 641.41–42). A cabby has a face like Henry Campbell. Parnell had gone under the aliases of Fox and Stewart and is said to be in South Africa, having changed his name to De Wet, the Boer general. When Stephen mentions John Bull, Bloom inquires "if it was John Bull the political celebrity of that ilk, as it struck him, the two identical names, as a striking coincidence" (*U* 662.10–12). Even the coffee and bun that Bloom and Stephen eat pass for drink and food in name only: "pushing the cup of what was temporarily supposed to be called coffee gradually nearer him" (*U* 622.38–39) and "pushing the socalled roll across" (*U* 623.2–3). Bloom himself temporarily becomes L. Boom as the result of a newspaper misprint. We cannot trust what we read. Nor can we trust what we hear. When Bloom hears Italian spoken (perhaps remembering Simon Dedalus' comment on Italian in "Sirens") he exclaims to Stephen, "A beautiful language. I mean for singing purposes. Why do you not write your poetry in that language? *Bella Poetria*! it is so melo-

---

2. See Marilyn French, *The Book as World* (Cambridge: Harvard University Press, 1976), 19. "'Eumaeus' offers deceits, errors, falsehoods. Not only the language but the events of the chapter are a network of deceits and errors. . . . It would seem that truths and falsehoods are equally dependable vehicles of the real."

dious and full. *Belladonna voglio*" (*U* 622.20–22). But the Italians he overhears are merely haggling over money.

Despite the fact that names and language are man's best means of establishing identity and truth, language itself becomes a pretender. "Eumaeus," which is presided over by Bloom's watered-down scientific skepticism ("he personally, being of a sceptical bias" [*U* 655.33–34]), is full of phrases making us question our trust in language and names. Here is a selection: "as they are called" (*U* 636.26), "or whatever you like to call it" (*U* 645.16), "tell a graphic lie" (*U* 647.8–9), "highly unlikely, of course, there was even a shadow of truth" (*U* 649.14–15), "sound the lie of the land" (*U* 650.22). Masquerading as a scene in Dublin, "Eumaeus" becomes a linguistic counterfeit exposing its own counterfeit.

Take, for instance, that pseudo-Ulysses figure D. B. Murphy, who in his own way dominates "Eumaeus."[3] The enigmatic Murphy first enters Bloom's and Stephen's conversation when, trusting sound and names too much, he mistakes Stephen's use of the name Murphy in the "what's in a name?" quotation for his own. "And what might your name be?" (*U* 623.7) he asks Stephen. When Stephen replies, "Dedalus," Murphy asks him if he knows Simon Dedalus. But our aroused expectations about Stephen's father are defeated; the Simon Dedalus whom Murphy knows works for a circus, Hengler's to be exact. Nor is Murphy's name to be trusted. Like most of the other characters, he may be operating under a pseudonym.

Detectivelike Bloom, who is said to be "Sherlockholmesing" (*U* 636.1) Murphy, discovers that the postcard Murphy passes around is addressed to "*Señor A. Boudin, Galeria Becche, Santiago, Chile*" (*U* 626.15–16). Though there was no "message" on the card, Bloom takes particular interest in Murphy's most-likely-fictional story, a story causing him to question Murphy's authenticity.

Though not an implicit believer in the lurid story narrated (or the eggsniping transaction for that matter despite William Tell and the Lazarillo-Don Cesar

3. See James H. Maddox, *Joyce's "Ulysses" and the Assault upon Character* (New Brunswick: Rutgers University Press, 1978), 157–64, who believes (as I do) that D. B. Murphy is another figure for Joyce. Maddox also recognizes that, throughout *Ulysses*, there are figures for Joyce "tucked away in a dark corner" but he dismisses these figures as "simply arabesques in the book's design" (96 n).

de Bazan incident depicted in *Maritana* on which occasion the former's ball passed through the latter's hat), having detected a discrepancy between his name (assuming he was the person he represented himself to be and not sailing under false colours after having boxed the compass on the strict q.t. somewhere) and the fictitious addressee of the missive which made him nourish some suspicions of our friend's *bona fides*, nevertheless it reminded him in a way of a longcherished plan he meant to one day realise some Wednesday or Saturday. (*U* 626.17–29).

In questioning Murphy's authenticity, Bloom questions his own, because he too receives letters under a pseudonym and false address. More important, Murphy's questionable tale casts doubt on the authenticity of the tale in which he and Bloom appear. This tale, *Ulysses*, is narrated by an "author" who within the story represents himself as a young man, Stephen Dedalus. But because our author is not "the person he represented himself to be," in fact is "sailing under false colours," we rightfully "nourish some suspicions of our friend's *bona fides*." Bloom, then, speaks with more wisdom than he thinks when he remarks, "Though in reality I'm not" (*U* 643.4).

Wielding his formidable stiletto, Joyce, like Adam, has the father's privilege to name those who reside in his paradise of pretenders.[4] Or, as Bloom says, "He had a capital opening to make a name for himself" (*U* 664.22–23). As the misprint of Bloom's name in the newspaper reminds us, the creator has the power to change a character's name at will. In fact, immediately after the misprint, the narrator of "Eumaeus" temporarily decides to refer to Bloom as Boom. "While the other was reading it on page two Boom (to give him for the nonce his new misnomer) whiled away a few odd leisure moments in fits and starts" (*U* 648.15–17). By the time that the narrator returns to Bloom's "real name," we realize that Bloom (who has also been called Virag, Leopold

---

4. Robert Kellogg, "Scylla and Charybdis," in Clive Hart and David Hayman (eds.), *James Joyce's "Ulysses"* (Berkeley: University of California Press, 1974), 162–63, provides a good passage on the use of proper names in that chapter, throughout which Stephen and the narrator use the artistic pseudonyms "A. E." and "Eglinton" to refer to two of the characters, and "the quaker librarian" to refer to another. But when the topic of the chapter turns to names, the "real" name and pseudonym come together: "Mageeglinjohn" (*U* 209.9) and "Quakerlyster" (*U* 209.29). Perhaps it is appropriate that Platonist A. E. has departed and is thus denied the substance of a "real" name.

M'Intosh, and Henry Flower) and all the other characters of the book depend upon the author for their names. Within the verbal universe of *Ulysses*, Joyce can choose names that take on symbolic meaning, so that the characters, like Bloom, are "properly so dubbed" (*U* 649.11). Coming as it does in the midst of "Eumaeus," where so many characters are mentioned with aliases or assumed identities (Parnell as Fox and Stewart, Tichborne's imposter, W. B. Murphy, Skin-the-Goat, Simon Dedalus of the circus), this commentary on naming forces us once again to confront the fact that the marks we read on the page are posing as words, the words are posing as fictional characters, and the fictional characters are posing as real people in Dublin, 16 June 1904.

Some critics, such as Robert Adams, have tried to underplay the importance of names in *Ulysses*, by pointing out that Joyce takes most of his names from real people. But Joyce accounts for such objections by having Stephen answer his critics in the library. "You will say those names were already in the chronicles from which he took the stuff of his plays. Why did he take them rather than others?" (*U* 211.28–30). As author, Joyce has free rein. If a name he finds in Thom's *Dublin Directory* is appropriate, so much the better; if not, Joyce can create a name of his own.

The result is the mixture of fact and fiction that continues to confuse so many readers. If Joyce warns us that what we are reading is fiction not fact, he continually insists on the ways in which they are interwoven. For example, in "Eumaeus" and *Ulysses* we have historical figures (Tichborne's imposter) masquerading as other historical figures; mythical figures (God as man) masquerading as historical; historical (Parnell) as mythical; fictional (all the characters in the book) as historical; and fictional (Simon Dedalus) as fictional (Simon Dedalus). History (16 June 1904) masquerades as myth and myth (the *Odyssey*) masquerades as history.

Joyce forces us to confront the blending of these two realms by having Bloom tell Stephen the story of his encounter with Parnell. "His hat (Parnell's) was inadvertently knocked off and, as a matter of strict history, Bloom was the man who picked it up in the crush after witnessing the occurrence meaning to return it to him (and return it to him he did with the utmost celerity)" (*U* 654.41–655.2). Here the realm of the fictional (as represented by Bloom) and the realm of the generally accepted historical (as represented by Parnell) clash, with unsettling consequences for the reader. Readers of *Ulysses* will gladly suspend their disbelief and accept the mention of "real" people and events in Joyce's fictional world. Joyce can even have characters like Parnell's brother or the vice-regent appear. But he cannot have a fictional character meet an important historical character and claim the meeting to be history without the reader's hedging. When the two realms meet, one response is for the reader to conclude "that a historical novel can never be history but is a fictional transposition of history into the realm of the imaginary."[5]

Yet, by having Bloom tell the incident as "a matter of strict history," Joyce reminds us that history, after all, is made up of stories told in books. As Stephen speculates while teaching history in "Nestor," "For them too history was a tale like any other too often heard" (*U* 25.12). Our knowledge of history comes, not from facts and events, but most often from written texts and documents that masquerade as objective records of events. Those texts, we are reminded, may be no better than "some scurrilous effusions from the facile pens of the O'Brienite scribes at the usual mudslinging occupation" (*U* 654.29–30).

It is not the simple case that words refuse to adhere to the real or that the real refuses to adhere to words. Our sense of the real depends on words and names, for it is the quality of language to suggest a reality at the same time that it announces its split from reality. The author has power over names at the same time that names control him and his sense of who he is.

To see the power of names we can return to the familiar case of M'Intosh. If Saussure thinks that names are different from ordinary nouns because they have a referent but signify no concept, what would he do with that ordinary noun *macintosh*, which is transformed into a name during the course of the book? M'Intosh, which as macintosh once had a referent and signified a concept, becomes an example of the split not only between signified and signifier but also between ref-

5. J. Hillis Miller, *The Form of Victorian Fiction* (Notre Dame: University of Notre Dame Press, 1968), 20.

erent and signifier. Our fascination with M'Intosh has to do with this gap, a gap that makes us want to find some significance in a name or at least in the act of naming.

By placing M'Intosh in the context of the pseudonyms of "Eumaeus," as Joyce does, he provides us with a few more hints about him, while letting M'Intosh teach us something about the nature of names. When the name M'Intosh appears in "Eumaeus" as part of the list of mourners at Dignam's funeral, the reader knows enough to see that anyone trying to reconstruct the events of this day would be misled by a newspaper's "objective" records. He would be misled because a name has the power to suggest a real person even though that suggestion is only a masquerade.

If we trust the meaning of macintosh before it becomes a proper name, M'Intosh seems to hide an identity rather than reveal one. A macintosh is an article of clothing that covers someone. Bloom, in fact, thinks of him late in "Ithaca" because he is gathering garments "multicoloured multiform multitudinous" (*U* 729.21). If a macintosh is a garment that covers, it seems to make sense that M'Intosh's name implies that there is someone behind the name to be dis-covered. But perhaps that is our problem. Perhaps there is nothing behind the macintosh to grasp. Perhaps M'Intosh is truly a case in which clothes make the man. Because M'Intosh's identity, like everything in a work of fiction, relies on a word, there is no "real" person beyond language to whom the word *M'Intosh* refers. If indeed there is nothing to be found under M'Intosh's coat of language, it seems to be wise to confine our investigations about him to the pure level of language, to realize that all that is in a name is a name. To be sure, it might be our fate never to escape the realm of language, since even what I have called identifying the "real" M'Intosh would involve giving him another name. The real significance of M'Intosh may be that it is a folly to search for a referent in a name, that for all the readers intent on trying to rename him he will remain what Joyce called him in his notes: Mockintosh.[6]

6. Frank Kermode, "The Man in the Macintosh, the Boy in the Shirt," in his *The Genesis of Secrecy: On the Interpretation of Narrative* (Cambridge: Harvard University Press, 1979), 49–73, uses the quest to identify M'Intosh as one of his examples of institutionalized exegesis, comparing it to the quest to identify the boy in Mark 14:51–52.

But such an answer is too simple. "The mocker is never taken seriously when he is most serious" (*U* 199.11–12). Even if we were to
deny a significance to M'Intosh's name, how about the act of naming?
The mere fact that M'Intosh is named seems to make him special.
Other mysterious figures walk the pages of *Ulysses* (the mystery man
on the beach, for instance), yet nameless they do not captivate our
interest as much as does M'Intosh. Indeed, in the context of Joyce's
works, the way in which M'Intosh receives his name does seem significant. He is named when Bloom fills a gap, a void, created by Hynes's
not finishing a sentence.

> And tell us, Hynes said, do you know that fellow in the, fellow was over
> there in the . . .
> He looked around.
> Macintosh. Yes, I saw him, Mr Bloom said. Where is he now?
> M'Intosh, Hynes said, scribbling, I don't know who he is. Is that his name?
> (*U* 112.4–10)

The way in which M'Intosh receives his name is one way of showing that filling in gaps in the text is accomplished only at the risk of
error and misinterpretation. We complete incomplete sentences with
words, but it is the nature of the word *macintosh* to cause confusion.
Bloom's macintosh turns into Hynes's M'Intosh, a verbal transformation that renders our attempt to achieve a tidy completion of Hynes's
sentence impossible. The moment we try to correct Hynes's mistake
by providing the real name of M'Intosh, we find ourselves repeating
the act by which he receives his original misnomer, that is, filling a gap
in the text. So, even though the *James Joyce Quarterly* recently published "A Final Note on M'Intosh,"[7] we will no more conclusively find
the real name of M'Intosh than we will find the correct word to define
Bloom's essence by completing his unfinished sentence on the beach:
"I AM A."

It is the nature of *Ulysses*, however, that our failures do not necessarily lead to nihilistic dead ends. They may be the source of perpetual
creation. It is, after all, the comic confusion of Bloom's and Hynes's

7. Lynn De Vore, "A Final Note on M'Intosh," *James Joyce Quarterly*, XVI (Spring,
1979), 347–50.

misunderstanding that gives birth to a literary character appropriately, if incorrectly, named M'Intosh. And it is that name, mistaken or not, that can launch our own creative endeavors. Launch them, that is, if we come to see that there is something more to a name than a name after all: namely, a name is not another name.

Rather than lamenting the fact that M'Intosh's misnomer hides his identity, we can be thankful that it at least suggests who he is not. While God can answer a question about his identity by responding, "I am who am," one thing we can be relatively certain of is that "M'Intosh" does not have the real name of M'Intosh. Nor is it likely that he is one of the other mourners at Dignam's funeral or one of the many characters mentioned in the last section of "Wandering Rocks." If calling M'Intosh M'Intosh does not satisfy our desire to know who he is, it at least distinguishes him from other characters named in the text. Nonetheless, because M'Intosh appears in *Ulysses*, it seems likely that he is a Dubliner or at least someone in Dublin, 16 June 1904. A good guess at M'Intosh's identity would be someone conspicuous by his absence from a list we could compile of characters in *Ulysses*.

Logic such as this has led a number of critics to identify M'Intosh as Mr. Duffy in "A Painful Case." Mr. Duffy seems a logical choice exactly because he is a character not mentioned in *Ulysses*, and yet one who would have a good reason to haunt the graveyard where Mrs. Sinico is buried. But the logic that suggests Mr. Duffy needs further refinement. M'Intosh is not only someone in Dublin absent from a list of characters in *Ulysses*; he is someone present in Dublin who, for some reason, cannot be given his proper name. Posed this way, the queston "Who was M'Intosh?" suggests a logical answer, but one that defies one of the most cherished conventions maintaining the all-too-easy distinction between fiction and reality. That convention tells us that of all the people walking around historical Dublin, 16 June 1904, the only one who could not appear as a character by name in a book written by James Joyce is the namer of all the other characters—Joyce himself. For Joyce, who has done such an excellent job of hiding himself behind a world of words, there could be few better disguises than wearing a macintosh, a cover that allows him to hide his own name behind the name of his cover. M'Intosh is an excellent pseudonym for an author.

So I am back to my original hypothesis: Joyce as M'Intosh. But our discussion of names puts us in a better position to see why that hypothesis will have to remain a hypothesis and why, even if we want to call M'Intosh Joyce, Joyce's return as M'Intosh is at best a ghostly return. If we ask again Shakespeare's and Stephen's question, "What's in a name?" we can answer: everything and nothing.

This is what Starobinski has to say about names:

We discover . . . that a man is never completely within his name, or completely behind his name, just as he is never completely within his face, or back of it. We cannot persevere very long in either the realistic or the nominative illusion. A name alternately appears as something full and something empty, in some cases fraught with great destiny of existence, in others reduced to a superficial and meaningless verbal convention. An entire life is concentrated in it as it is reduced to a symbol. But this symbol is only a symbol, we can learn nothing from it. We no longer know before whom we stand.[8]

While I agree with Starobinski that we no longer know before whom we stand, I do not agree that we can learn nothing from a name. A name, I submit, can help us learn something about the nature of names. Since names are not separate from our sense of reality but part (not all) of it, that is no small lesson.

If, for instance, we accept for a moment the hypothesis that I and others have advanced, that M'Intosh may be a figure for Joyce, we can see how M'Intosh illustrates the qualities of a pseudonym as outlined by Starobinski. According to Starobinski, when someone adopts a pseudonym, he repudiates the name transmitted by his father. "In giving himself a pseudonym, he affirms his basic autonomy."[9] By becoming his own namer, he tries to become the author of his own destiny. Interestingly enough, the etymology of the word *macintosh* is that it is named after its inventor. And if M'Intosh is a figure for Joyce, Joyce adds the special touch that he receives his name from one of his fictional characters, temporarily adopting the role of author to name one of his other characters.

A pseudonym not only indicates a desire to rupture paternal origin, it also indicates a desire to lessen the control of others over us. Since others know us through our name, to be confined to our given

8. Starobinski, "Truth in Masquerade," 116.
9. *Ibid.*, 117.

name means that our identity comes to us through and from others. "Our identity which binds us to our name, delivers us at the same time as hostages to other consciences." The adopter of a pseudonym "cannot prevent the world from using his name, but he can arrange for his name to cease designating him. He dreams somewhat ingeniously of being in the situation of seeing without being seen." We are reminded at once of Bloom, writing a letter to Martha in "Sirens" under the pseudonym of Henry Flower, wanting to "see, not be seen" (*U* 265.17). Equally important is M'Intosh's escape into invisibility. As Phillip Herring points out, in the notebook for "Hades" the word *Tarnkappe* appears. *Tarnkappe*, which in German means a cloak of invisibility, probably refers to M'Intosh's cover. The verb *tarnen* means to camouflage, mask, or screen.[10]

Most of all, of course, M'Intosh's identity is screened from the reader. While traditionally macintoshes are worn by detectives, in *Ulysses* the reader becomes a detective as he tries to track down clues that will allow him to uncover the identity of the man in the mac. Very likely, however, he is on a hopeless wild-goose chase after an Irish wild goose.

If the other pseudonyms appearing in "Eumaeus" are not warning enough, the case of M'Intosh seems to remind us of the split between signifier and referent. This split has important implications for Joyce's return to the world of his text through the act of writing. The signatures of all things that make up a literary text do not incarnate the presence of their author. The nature of language undercuts any return he might make except the return as a ghost. To borrow a structuralist's way of putting it: " 'I' is therefore in the 'texts,' but not as a subject at their origin—that is to say, not as their 'author'—but as their object, the one who must be sought precisely because he is absent from them. Yet it is vain to attempt to discover him for the very reason that he is indeed absent."[11] The signatures he leaves behind record his absence, yet his absence hauntingly suggests his presence.

10. *Ibid.*; Phillip Herring, *Joyce's Notes and Early Drafts for "Ulysses"* (Charlottesville: University Press of Virginia, 1977), 8.

11. Jacques Ehrmann, "The Death of Literature," *New Literary History*, III (Autumn, 1971), 35.

The case of M'Intosh is a perfect example of a word reaching out to name a presence (perhaps even the author himself) only to turn back on itself, announcing its existence as a sign. In a literary text we are left with a world of words. Thus, the easiest way to track down M'Intosh's appearance in *Ulysses* is to consult the *Word Index*. But as the name Joyce chose for his mystery man shows, words themselves are protean; macintosh becomes M'Intosh becomes mackintosh becomes Mackintosh. Critics, among them Phillip Herring and Frank Kermode, have even added another spelling: MacIntosh.

Indeed, it is exactly because with M'Intosh we do not know before whom we stand that the name M'Intosh helps teach us something about the world of words he inhabits. And it is important for readers of *Ulysses* to remember that the question that encourages the search after M'Intosh's identity is itself an answer.

> What selfinvolved enigma did Bloom risen, going, gathering multicoloured multiform multitudinous garments, voluntarily apprehending, not comprehend?
> Who was M'Intosh? (*U* 729.20–23)

It is not surprising that a question, coming late in "Ithaca," should be answered by another question, for by now we have been led to see the limitations of the question-and-answer method, which assumes that for each question there is a definite answer. Instead of providing answers to all its questions, the chapter shows that the answers we come up with depend on the questions we raise. To point to one obvious example, I come up with the hypothesis that M'Intosh is Joyce because of the way I pose the question: Who was M'Intosh? Others, less concerned with identifying M'Intosh as someone who might have been in Dublin on 16 June 1904, can identify him as death, Hades, or the risen Christ.

The way in which the type of questions we ask determines the answers we come up with is made "clearer" in the next question-and-answer pair, which also has a question for an answer.

> What selfevident enigma pondered with desultory constancy during 30 years did Bloom now, having effected natural obscurity by the extinction of artificial light, silently suddenly comprehend?
> Where was Moses when the candle went out? (*U* 729.24–28)

Questions, like this second answer-as-question, with self-evident answers do not lead us very far; we are still left in the dark. On the other hand, questions, like the first, while still leaving us in the dark, because they have no self-evident answers, help illuminate many details that we might never have bothered to ask about, even if it is in the nature of those details to raise more questions. The name M'Intosh does not lead us securely to an identity; instead it turns us to a never-ending odyssey through the book's pages. Perhaps the best solution to the identity of M'Intosh is to eliminate the question mark at the end of the question and turn the answer into a statement: Who was M'Intosh.[12]

But why all this attention to M'Intosh? Is not M'Intosh a special case? Only in a sense. As I have suggested, in the context of "Eumaeus" the questions about M'Intosh's name are perfectly normal. And once alerted to the nature of names in "Eumaeus," we can turn to the rest of the book and find the same qualities there.

Throughout the day identities and names are confused, lost, or forgotten. In "Lotus Eaters" the case of M'Intosh is anticipated when the name of an object turns into a proper name—Throwaway. Earlier in the chapter it is revealed that Bloom adopts a pseudonym in his correspondence with Martha Clifford. It is not until later that we learn that Martha may not be the person she represents herself to be. Martha Clifford may be as bogus a name as Henry Flower.[13] In "Cyclops" we have a surplus of names in the many lists, including the names of "real" people. Meanwhile, almost all the "real" characters are referred to by initials or nicknames, rarely "proper" names. The narrator, of course, is completely nameless. "Circe" is full of changes of name, costume, and identity. At the end of the chapter, Bloom creates a new character for the book from the world of art when he hears Stephen drunkenly reciting "Who goes with Fergus" and imagines "Ferguson, I think I caught. A girl. Some girl. Best thing could happen him" (*U* 609.11–13). On the other hand, earlier in the book the blind stripling

12. Sean Golden suggested this to me in conversation after a talk at the Joyce meeting in Provincetown, Massachusetts, 15 June 1980.
13. Michael Begnal, "The Unveiling of Martha Clifford," *James Joyce Quarterly*, XIII (Summer, 1976), 400–406.

has gone unnamed, even though Bloom ponders, "Wonder if he has a name" (*U* 181.16). We might also wonder about the real name of the first character we meet, and I do not mean Oliver Saint John Gogarty. In "Oxen of the Sun" we are given the name "Malachi Roland St John Mulligan" (*U* 417.40). But is the prose of "Oxen" to be trusted? Doesn't Buck's name sound a bit "high," as Joyce described the chapter to Budgen? Elsewhere, do we have Pendennis or Penrose? Kendal Bushe or Seymour Bushe? Sidney Lee or Simon Lazarus? Purefoy or Beaufoy? Crofton or Crofter or Crawford?

Names are easily confused, and works of art do not undo the confusion. In "Hades," the chapter in which M'Intosh is named, another story about mistaken identity is told. This time the confusion is caused by a work of art and people's desire for realism.

They tell the story, he said, that two drunks came out here one foggy evening to look for the grave of a friend of theirs. They asked for Mulcahy from the Coombe and were told where he was buried. After traipsing about in the fog they found the grave, sure enough. One of the drunks spelt out the name: Terence Mulcahy. The other drunk was blinking up at a statue of our Saviour the widow had got put up.

The caretaker blinked up at one of the sepulchres they passed. He resumed:

And, after blinking up at the sacred figure, *Not a bloody bit like the man,* says he. *That's not Mulcahy,* says he, *whoever done it.* (*U* 107.13–24)

There are readers who try to identify Bloom and M'Intosh as the Savior or, if not the Savior, at least Odysseus. A comparison of M'Intosh with Odysseus can help us better understand what we are doing when we make such identifications.

M'Intosh, as a name, has more in common with the first name we encounter in the book, its title, than we might think. We have already seen how Ulysses is conspicuous in the book by his total absence except his identification, macintoshlike, on its cover. While with M'Intosh we are confronted with a character without a proper name (our task is to find a name to fit the character), with Ulysses we have a name but no character (our task is to find a character to fit the name). But like M'Intosh, Joyce's Ulysses never reveals who he is. In fact, if it were not for the book's critical tradition, much of it directed by Joyce himself, by the time we reach "Ithaca" a question a reader might as easily pose as "Who was M'Intosh?" would be, Who was Ulysses? We have, after all, been reading for over seven hundred pages and the title character has yet to make an appearance. Joyce could have made this question unnecessary by affixing the name of Ulysses to a character and by having him walk the pages of his book, a strategy adopted by three of his favorite writers—Dante, Shakespeare, and Hauptmann. But it is Ulysses' absence that gives the book one of its most important effects: an infinite series of potential connections between Dublin, 16 June 1904, and the *Odyssey*, connections that we discover by asking questions implied by a name, a name that from the Greek can be translated as trouble.[14]

Hugh Kenner compares the title of *Ulysses* to a metal plate in the Vatican from which we can view Bernini's elliptical colonnade, to make two redundant rows of columns disappear.[15] Acting as such a metal plate, the book's title allows us a perspective from which we can align Joyce's tale with the *Odyssey*. That alignment arranges seemingly random details into meaningful patterns and gives the book a sense of order. But the alignment in *Ulysses* is not achieved as automatically as standing on a metal plate. For one, it does not work unless we identify our title character. Could Ulysses be the first character we meet, Buck Mulligan, who plays so well the role of a Ulysses-like trickster? Or Stephen Dedalus, who, despite announcing early that "I'm not a hero" (*U* 4.29), performs the heroic stunt of intellectually steering between Scylla and Charybdis? Or even D. B. Murphy, a wandering sailor returned home to Dublin? Of course, none of these characters fits the role as convincingly as our modern-day Odysseus, Leopold Bloom. But what are we doing when we identify Bloom as Odysseus? The Bloom / Odysseus alignment is by no means a perfect one.

A perfect alignment would imply an identity; the book's action would coincide with the book's title; Bloom would equal Ulysses. But the connections between Joyce's tale and Homer's tale never quite meet. While Fritz Senn points to *Ulysses*' Odyssean nature by describ-

14. George E. Dimock, Jr., "The Name of Odysseus," *Hudson Review*, IX (Spring, 1956), 57.

15. Hugh Kenner, *Joyce's Voices* (Berkeley: University of California Press, 1978), 60.

ing it as polytropic, part of its polytropic nature is that it leads Senn to refine his description by referring to another classical text. Rather than a book in which identities are achieved, *"Ulysses* is Joyce's *Metamorphoses*, a book of roles and guises, a game of identities, of transubstantiations."[16] Significantly, in this book of many turns, it is a name promising an identity that provides the book with its first turn—its first trope. When the reader turns from the title page to the first page, he finds a book not about Homer's Greece but about twentieth-century Dublin. Rather than serving as an identification, the book's title serves as a metaphor, offering metaphors by which we can read it, such as a book of many turns or a book as an odyssey. The name Ulysses can no more establish an identity with certainty than can the name M'Intosh. Ulysses, which is the Roman name of a character who is a secondhand version of Homer's original, turns into, but is not identical with, a twentieth-century Dublin Jew named Leopold Bloom.

Totally to identify Bloom with Ulysses is to make an alignment with only one eye open. When we open the other, the alignment goes astray, even though we now see Bloom more fully, since what we have come to call Bloom's identity is established as much by the ways in which he is not Ulysses as by the ways in which he is. Thus, like M'Intosh, the name Ulysses helps suggest through indirection—that way all tropes turn. The mere fact that the name Ulysses is available helps us create Bloom, for he would be quite different if we did not make the comparison the title invites. Ulysses makes his presence felt, by remaining absent. It is we, invited by another absent figure—James Joyce—who make Ulysses present.

As should be clear by now, when I suggest that we might call M'Intosh Joyce, I have in mind the way in which we call Bloom Ulysses. M'Intosh is Joyce and he is not Joyce. To call him Joyce sets up an alignment that helps order some unexplained details in the book. The moment we try to pin that identity down, we find the person we have come to call Joyce eluding our grasp and once again fading into absence. But what should be clearer by now is how important absences are in *Ulysses*, for a principle of this book, which has so often been

16. Fritz Senn, "Book of Many Turns," *James Joyce Quarterly*, X (Fall, 1972), 31.

praised as encyclopedic, is that the questions and answers we come up with are conditioned by absences.

Perfect alignments imply presences not absences. But in a world in which signified and signifier and referent do not coincide, such alignments are not possible. I have tried to show that, even in the special case of proper names, there is no natural connection between name and referent. If even names turn out to be tropes, providing metaphors but not identities, we can better understand what is involved in the reading process of *Ulysses*.

Whenever we identify a character or a world in the act of reading, we are turning absences into presences. The words of *Ulysses* do not establish a one-to-one correspondence with a preexisting reality any more than the marks of paint on a canvas do. As E. H. Gombrich has convincingly demonstrated for the world of visual arts, the creation of an illusion of reality depends as much on the artist's appealing to the conventions by which a viewer has come to see "reality" as on his establishing a connection between his canvas and a world beyond his canvas. "Once this fact is understood it may be easier to see why the amount of information packed into the picture may hinder the illusion as frequently as it helps it. The reason lies precisely in the limitations of the medium that may occasionally obtrude themselves and contradict the impression the painter wanted to conjure up. No wonder, therefore, that the greatest protagonist of naturalistic illusion in painting, Leonardo da Vinci, is also the innovator of the deliberately blurred image, the *sfumato*, or veiled form, that cuts down the information on the canvas and thereby stimulates the mechanism of projections."[17]

By stimulating the viewer's mechanism of projection, art has the power to suggest what is not there. Empty space in many Chinese paintings becomes something. Two feet and hands protruding from behind the cross in Giotto's *Last Judgment* suggest an unseen figure. While Gombrich does not risk describing exactly what mental process is involved in creating these illusions, he does give an example. He refers to "the type of lettering known as Shadow Antiqua ('Granby Shadow'), in which the familiar forms of letters are only indicated by

17. E. H. Gombrich, *Art and Illusion* (London: Phaidon Press, 1972), 185.

what would be the shaded side if they were formed of ribbons standing up. The distance between the shades indicates there is a slight band
along the thickness of the ribbon. There is no such band, but many
observers see it running along the whole top of the letter."[18]

ILLUSION

In *Ulysses* the sense of the real that readers believe in also depends
on techniques of suggestion. Despite its apparent comprehensiveness,
Ulysses has as many blank spaces as does a Chinese painting. Because
the chapters do not link to one another in a smooth chronological order, we are left with blank spaces during the day, about some of which
implications are thickly scattered. Equally important, the sheer number of styles itself creates the illusion that more happens than the language records. It has become fashionable to praise the book's initial
style for its objectivity. Yet it is this style that, through its famous interior monologue, is most firmly lodged within a character's consciousness, be it Stephen's or Bloom's. Once we realize that what we are
given is not an objective account of a Dublin reality but someone's
interpretation of it, we are in a better position to see that all the
book's styles are interpretive schemas, ways of seeing the world, not
the world itself. Since choosing one style assumes interpretive schemas that another style excludes, Joyce's encyclopedia of styles creates
the illusion that language reaches out to "capture" a reality, but re-
peatedly falls short.

Trying to explain this effect, Arnold Goldman claims that the
book's styles suggest the existence of a noumenal level of action.

Ulysses seems to posit a *noumenal* level which does not deny the multiplicity
of phenomenal interpretive ones, but which is behind and beyond them, necessary to them inasmuch as without it, they could not exist at all. As *Ulysses*
proceeds, the phenomenal dimension discovers that it can enjoy itself almost,
as it were, at the expense of the noumenal one, but only at the cost of re-

18. *Ibid.*, 210.

linquishing a denominative, or final interpretation of it. . . . The method of *Ulysses* is an accommodation of the total potentiality of a subject and the particular version(s) of it brought into being. *Ulysses* is most particularly an encyclopaedic fiction in this respect.[19]

I would put this a different way. Joyce's multiplicity of styles creates the conditions necessary to produce an illusion that an external reality to be portrayed exists independently of the styles themselves. It even suggests events belonging to this reality that happen "offstage," outside the book's explicit mention. As we have seen, Joyce, by successfully creating this illusion of an independent reality, leads critics to talk about the inadequacy of a certain style to capture the essence of Bloom or to talk about a style screening us from the book's action or to search after the real identity of M'Intosh. But the point remains that there is no action independent of the book's styles. Joyce's supreme achievement is creating the illusion of a subject matter that does not exist.

To talk of a subject matter that does not exist is not to indulge in inconsistencies. It is merely to emphasize the fact that *Ulysses'* subject matter exists not as the representation of some independent reality but as an imaginative construct in words, created first by Joyce and then by the reader. Nonetheless, to someone within the empirical tradition, the idea of a subject matter that does not exist can cause confusion. In the Lockean tradition, even an idea is something that imprints itself on the mind. Thus, in Joycean criticism, it has taken the work of Wolfgang Iser, a German critic within the phenomenological tradition, to explain most accurately the effect of Joyce's techniques of suggestion. In writing about a novel's subject matter that exists only as an absence, Iser distinguishes between *Wahrnehmen* and *Vorstellen*. *Wahrnehmen*, which corresponds to the English "perception," requires the actual presence of an object; *Vorstellen*, for which there is no accurate English equivalent, depends on the absence or "not-givenness" of an object.[20] *Vorstellen*, therefore, allows us to speak of those

19. Arnold Goldman, *The Joyce Paradox* (Evanston: Northwestern University Press, 1968), 95. Goldman's position has become increasingly influential. Maddox, *Joyce's "Ulysses" and the Assault upon Character*, 168, quotes this passage and relates it to French's position.
20. Wolfgang Iser, *The Act of Reading* (Baltimore: Johns Hopkins University Press,

activities of the mind that do not depend on the existence of an empirical object, without considering these activities, as they often are in the Lockean tradition, merely imaginary or fanciful. *Vorstellen*, in fact, is a very real mental activity, since it is one of the ways by which the mind has access to the world. It is certainly a mental activity that helps the reader turn words into worlds.

Joyce, it seems, was aware of the reader's role in fiction from the start. Even in his so-called naturalistic stories, Joyce does not present a completed reality that the reader can passively consume. Instead he presents an opportunity for the reader to create an illusion of reality. On the first page of "The Sisters," Joyce's first work of fiction, the narrator mentions the gnomon from Euclid, a geometric figure that suggests a parallelogram despite being incomplete. As a physical object, a gnomon also serves as an indicator by casting a shadow. Specifically, mention of the gnomon comments on the technique of "The Sisters." We can only approach an understanding of the story when we complete the incomplete sentences with which it ends.[21] As readers, we are forced to make meaning out of the substance of the shadows cast by the finely chiseled details of its prose. But more generally the gnomon casts a shadow that anticipates the technique employed in all Joyce's work to come. The words on the page do not name an already existing reality. Instead they suggest a reality that exists only as an absence. From this absence we as readers create the actions of the text. By using the tale of the telling deliberately to destroy the book's carefully constructed illusion of reality, by emphasizing the materiality of language, by foregrounding the play of language, by drawing attention

---

1978), 136–37. It is useful to compare the English version with the original, *Der Akt des Lesens* (Munich: Wilhelm Fink, 1976), 222–24. Iser used the *Wahrnehmen-Vorstellen* distinction to respond to his German critics: see his "Im Lichte der Kritik," in Rainer Warning (ed.), *Rezeptionsästhetik* (Munich: Wilhelm Fink, 1975), 326–27.

21. Many have commented on the incomplete sentences of "The Sisters." One of the first was Fritz Senn, "He Was Too Scrupulous Always: Joyce's 'The Sisters,'" *James Joyce Quarterly*, II (Winter, 1965), 66–71. On the gnomon in this context, see Shari Benstock, "*Ulysses* as Ghoststory," *James Joyce Quarterly*, XII (Summer, 1975), 398–400. The most comprehensive look at "The Sisters" is Thomas F. Staley, "A Beginning: Signification, Story, and Discourse in Joyce's 'The Sisters,'" *Genre*, XII (Winter, 1979), 533–48.

to the act of naming, Joyce reminds the reader of his role as an accomplice in giving the book life.

If the world of time denies Bloom a successful return home because it leaves a gap that does not allow a circle to close and if the temporal nature of language denies Joyce a successful return to his text because there is always a gap between signified and signifier, these gaps allow the reader to make many happy returns to the book's pages. It is the tropological nature of the book's language continually turning away from presence that causes the reader to have an odyssey with no ends, only turns and returns. That odyssey deserves a closer look.

Part III

The Royal Reader

Chapter Five

History Repeating Itself with a Difference

Perhaps the best way to start describing the reader's odyssey is to return to the author's odyssey in writing *Ulysses*. I say this because one of the most interesting results of the current fascination with reader-response criticism may turn out paradoxically to be an explanation of what, for lack of a better term, we call the creativity of writers such as James Joyce. Of course, normally reader-oriented criticism is applied to the role of the reader in literature. Rejecting the textual model that emphasizes the active role of the writer in producing a text and the passive role of the reader in reproducing it, the advocates of reader-response criticism remind those who need reminding that reading is not merely a passive process. The reader's activity varies from theory to theory, from a reader "adducing" meaning to a reader "producing" meaning, but in almost all cases the reader is seen more and more as an accomplice in the creation of the meaning of a text, a necessary partner who re-creates or, for some, "re-writes" the text.

For me, however, the converse of the argument is just as interesting. If reading is shown to be a form of writing, writing is also shown to be a form of reading. Just as reading is no longer considered merely a passive process, so writing is no longer considered a totally active process. Instead writing itself is shown to involve an act of passivity. As we often tell students of composition, writing is a continued process of revision, and as that master of the craft, Henry James, put it: "To revise is to see, or to look over again—which means in the case of a written thing neither more nor less than to re-read it."[1]

This merger of the roles of reader and writer is perhaps no better in evidence than in the case of Joyce and *Ulysses*. With the widespread availability of Joyce's notesheets and revisions for *Ulysses*, plus Michael Groden's detailed study of Joyce's process of writing the book, we have a privileged opportunity to watch closely how one of the twentieth century's most creative users of language wrote his masterpiece. What we find is that Joyce's continual reading and rereading of what he had already written more than anything explain why *Ulysses*, which started as a short story for *Dubliners*, kept expanding until Joyce finally had to stop adding to it to meet the publication deadline on his fortieth birthday. As one of Joyce's late revisions proclaims, "*It grew bigger and bigger and bigger*" (*U* 172.36). Joyce, the writer, was such a sensitive reader of his own work that he continually detected new verbal connections and possibilities to be developed in rewriting.

Because Joyce's composition of *Ulysses* was so complicated, the precise details of his writing, reading, rewriting, and rereading are impossible to recover. We could point to certain obvious moments, such as when he most likely reread drafts of the early chapters before sending them to the *Little Review*. This rereading could have influenced his move from the book's initial style to its stylistic experimentations. Someone as sensitive as Joyce to narrative possibilities would soon see the limitations of any one style, including the famous interior monologue, which, once considered a major deviation from narrative norms, is now grasped at by critics seeking to define *Ulysses'* stylistic norm. It is important to remember, however, that not only do the later chapters of the book grow out of and depend on the earlier ones, but by the time *Ulysses* reaches print the earlier have been somewhat revised in light of the later. These revisions could be traced to Joyce's meticulous rereading of his entire book in proof, a rereading that, significantly, was not done in a linear fashion.

1. Henry James, *The Art of the Novel* (New York: Scribners, 1934), 338–39. See Walter Benn Michaels, "Writers Reading: James and Eliot," *Modern Language Notes*, XCI (October, 1976), 827–49, for a valuable discussion of James's theory of reading.

Nonetheless, to point to such acts would be to risk forgetting that Joyce's reading and rereading were a continuous process, by no means confined to specific moments. As Groden argues, Joyce's strategies and intentions changed and developed as he wrote and read his book, until he created a final draft that would be "a record of all of the stages he passed through and not merely a product of the last one."[2] Joyce's process of writing makes possible a perpetual interaction between all the book's chapters, styles, and words.

Thus, complaints about Joyce's overly mechanical structure might be reconsidered. Joyce did not simply impose a mechanical structure on the work, since the various structures that he himself discovered grew out of the act of composition. For instance, the famous schema did not appear until late in Joyce's work on the book, indicating that he may not have seen the possibility for many of his elaborate, encyclopedic parallels until after the book amassed more and more words. In fact, as Groden points out, a comparison of the Linati schema with the Stuart Gilbert schema indicates that the schema itself was revised to fit new work on the book. Furthermore, it is typical of Joyce that what Joseph Frank calls the book's spatial structure grew out of the artist's writing process. It is Joyce's continual revisions that gave the book the appearance of having a preconceived structure in which all the details fit neatly together. And it is, of course, the book's "spatial" character that allows the reader to participate in a reading *process* with no end, jumping from page to page, reading both backwards and forwards. Frank wrote long ago that *Ulysses* cannot be read, only re-read.[3]

A good place to watch Joyce as the reader and the writer of his own work is once again "Eumaeus." Of all the chapters in *Ulysses*, "Eu-

2. See Hans Walter Gabler, "Shaping His Text to His Oeuvre: The Emergence of *Ulysses*," to appear in a centenary volume on Joyce edited by Hugh Kenner and Thomas Staley, published by University of California Press. Michael Groden, *"Ulysses" in Progress* (Princeton: Princeton University Press, 1977), 203. Michael Groden (ed.), *The James Joyce Archive* (New York: Garland Press, 1978), which reproduces all extant documents for *Ulysses*, provides evidence for the revisions I cite.

3. Joseph Frank, "Spatial Forms in Modern Literature," in Mark Schorer, Josephine Miles, and Gordon McKenzie (eds.), *Criticism* (New York: Harcourt, Brace & World, 1958), 385.

maeus" has the distinction of being its most maligned. Confronted with what they feel is the chapter's tired prose, many critics explain it away as the result of the fallacy of imitative form (tired prose to reflect Bloom's tired state of mind) or as the result of Joyce's own fatigue after long months of struggle with "Circe." But another look at the chapter, especially the revisions, shows that Joyce was not nodding. He wrote, reread, and rewrote this chapter with as much care as any other.

If the reader can wake himself from a sleep similar to the one that overtook Odysseus upon his return to Ithaca, he will discover that Bloom is not intellectually tired in "Eumaeus" after all. All day he has been searching for an audience worthy of his sensitive mind. Finally he thinks he has found it in Stephen. While Stephen may very well be exhausted—for the first time all day he abandons his exalted literary style—Bloom swarms with energy. The style of "Eumaeus" approximates the style Bloom would like to adopt to impress his companion in intellect. As Bloom's ideal of "fine writing—perhaps the style he would use to write *My Experiences in a Cabman's Shelter*—it represents a linguistic evocation of Bloom as important in its way as the celebrated interior monologue. It shows both Bloom's strength and his weakness. His strength lies in his unfailing mental energy; the style shows a mind gushing forth, trying to express sophisticated ideas. His weakness is that he lacks the linguistic resources to shape those ideas; the literary discourse available to Bloom takes over, resulting in prose that sprawls all over the page, full of comic qualifications and reversals.

One technique available to Bloom to achieve a literary style is to elevate it with what H. W. Fowler calls elegant variation. So in "Eumaeus" we watch the prose straining to find alternatives for "he said." The result: one page (*U* 619) includes "he also remarked" (.2), "testifying" (.3), "he said, laughingly" (.16), "he asked" (.18), "he observed evasively" (.25–26), "he queried" (.29), "Stephen responded" (.31), "Mr Bloom ejaculated" (.33), "added he with a smile" (.37), and "was Stephen's answer" (.43). The narrator allots the pedestrian "he said, laughingly" and "was Stephen's answer" to Stephen and gives Bloom more literary terms. In fact, in their direct speeches Stephen uses the flat "he asked," while Bloom uses the more eloquent "he queried."

A quick glance at the revisions Joyce made as the chapter grew from written manuscript to final text affirms that he knew exactly what he was up to in fancifying a style to conform to Bloom's critical sense. For instance, "interpolated" (*U* 629.42), "coined" (*U* 636.21), "dittoed" (*U* 637.22), and "to stipulate" (*U* 643.14) replace, respectively, "said," "told," "agreed," and "to say." Names are also circumlocutory; so "the more experienced of the two" (*U* 634.20) and "his good genius" (*U* 635.19) replace "Mr. Bloom"; "his companion" (*U* 648.4) replaces "Stephen" and "our hero" (*U* 658.26), "he." Bloom's dialogue itself is made more Bloomesque by an advertising diction. Thus, "a revolution must come bit by bit" turns into "a revolution must come on the due instalments plan" (*U* 643.22–23). Revising the phrase to match the advertising lingo of Bloom goes hand in hand with Joyce's desire throughout *Ulysses* to rely on concrete over abstract words, but here even the concrete words wallow in cliché. In fact, "made tracks" for "walked" (*U* 638.22), "have a shot at it" for "try it" (*U* 635.13), and "not being up to the scratch" for "not being up to much" (*U* 651.14) lodge the style more firmly in the realm of Bloom's "locutions reçues." Finally, imagine Joyce's delight when he saw a chance to *add* to the manuscript, "To cut a long story short" (*U* 659.40).

Critics who condemn such a style for its clichés miss the play of language that is activated upon rereading. Reread, seemingly dead language can be given new life, often by having the reader return to the words' old meanings that comically clash with their present sense. As Fritz Senn remarks, "Part of the dynamism of Joyce's prose arises from the contrast of figurative to literal meaning, or the ironic unfittingness of a metaphor or a cliché fixed in some no longer congruous roles."[4] We can observe this dynamism at work by examining one passage closely.

As D. B. Murphy spins story after story, Bloom considers the possibility that these stories might after all have a bit of truth in them. "Yet still, though his eyes were thick with sleep and sea air, life was full of a host of things and coincidences of a terrible nature and it was

4. Fritz Senn, "Book of Many Turns," *James Joyce Quarterly*, X (Fall, 1972), 42.

quite within the bounds of possibility that it was not an entire fabrication though at first blush there was not much inherent probability in all the spoof he got off his chest being strictly accurate gospel" (*U* 635.37–42). Rereading this passage, we might consider what Murphy quite literally has on his chest, although to do so will involve us in a series of not so literal connections with other parts of the text. What we find is that when Murphy unbuttons his shirt, he reveals, "on top of the timehonoured symbol of the mariner's hope and rest . . . the figure 16 and a young man's sideface looking frowningly rather" (*U* 631.21–22, 23–24). The young man's face turns out to be none other than a portrait of the tattoo artist himself—"fellow the name of Antonio done that. There he is himself, a Greek" (*U* 631.27–28). In other words, this "not entire fabrication" that our storyteller is trying to get off his chest is a portrait of the artist with a Greek name as a young man, a connection between Joyce and his fictional character that is reinforced later in the chapter when we are explicitly warned not to confuse Antonio with "the dramatic personage of identical name who sprang from the pen of our national poet" (*U* 636.11–12).[5] So warned, we immediately look for a connection. Literally, of course, this phrase refers to a character in Shakespeare's *Merchant of Venice*, but it also suggests Ireland's new national poet.

Furthermore, as Worton David and Harry Fragson point out, the song about the ice-cream vendor Antonio that Bloom has remembered in "Hades" is a modern version of Shylock's speech to Antonio.[6] So, mention of Antonio sends us flipping pages back to "Hades" and Bloom's "Has anybody here seen Kelly? Kay ee double ell wy. Dead march from *Saul*. He's as bad as old Antonio. He left me on my ownio" (*U* 97.20–22). If Antonio is one aspect of Ireland's national poet, then he certainly has left Bloom, one of his fictional characters, temporarily to walk the pages of *Ulysses* on his ownio. The song Bloom remembers links Antonio to another cluster of associations, because a few pages later Bloom repeats the line, "Kay ee double ell. Become invisi-

5. James H. Maddox, *Joyce's "Ulysses" and the Assault upon Character* (New Brunswick: Rutgers University Press, 1978), 159–60, also sees Murphy's tattoo as a portrait of the artist.
6. Ruth H. Bauerle, *The James Joyce Songbook* (New York: Garland Press, forthcoming).

ble" (U 112.14–15). This time the reference is to the mysterious man in the macintosh and his sudden disappearance at the funeral. The portrait of the artist Murphy uncovers is an interesting one indeed.

The path we follow in tracking down the connections that Murphy's tattoo suggests has been charted before. It is similar to the one Joyce took in creating them. Both of the passages I quote from "Hades" are late revisions, put in, no doubt, as a way of creating this elaborate series of connections. Nor should we be surprised to find that the key phrase that sets our journey in motion, "all the spoof he got off his chest being strictly accurate gospel," is a late revision. In the manuscript version that we have, Joyce ends the sentence with the rather bland "though at first blush there was not much inherent probability about it," with "inherent" a marginal addition. In the typescript, he revised this to "though at first blush there was not much inherent probability in all he said being strictly accurate," a change that emphasizes the act of narration and makes possible a further revision that will include the reference to Murphy's tatto, as well as allowing the addition of "gospel" to reinforce the effect of "host" earlier in the sentence. Host and gospel in turn connect the passage to Stephen's and Bloom's comments, on the previous page, about those "passages in Holy Writ" that Stephen calls proof of "the existence of a supernatural God" and Bloom considers "genuine forgeries (another late revision) "put in by monks most probably." Reference to monks recalls Old Monks, the dayfather in "Aeolus," who as James H. Maddox remarks "might well serve as a model of Joyce, dayfather of June 16, 1904."[7] Perhaps it is when Monks is interrupted, as he is in "Aeolus," that the newspaper "forgery" of L. Boom for Bloom occurs (see U 121.30). To be sure, Bloom's thoughts about the dayfather could apply as easily to Joyce as to Old Monks. "Queer lot of stuff he must have put through his hands in his time: obituary notices, pubs' ads, speeches, divorce suits, found drowned" (U 122.8–11). It is materials like these that make up "a host of things and coincidences of a terrible nature" that, like Ulysses, constitutes not an entire fabrication but a series of things that actually happened in Dublin.

7. Maddox, Joyce's "Ulysses" and the Assault upon Character, 95.

What my example, which is by no means unusual, should make clear is that Joyce's process of writing, rereading, and rewriting is potentially an endless one. Having once revised a passage, Joyce would reread his revisions, causing him to discover even more potential verbal connections, causing more rewriting, and so on.

Once we are made aware of Joyce's continual process of rewriting, it is easy to see how *Ulysses* came to be more and more about its own creation. Groden suggests that the *"Done"* (U 291.13) at the end of "Sirens" announces the end of Joyce's experimentation with the "initial style." He also remarks, "It is probably not coincidental that, just as Joyce was about to expand *Ulysses* through innumerable revisions, he wrote a scene extending Bloom's dreams to apocalyptic dimensions."[8] I also like to think that the trial scene in "Circe" owes something to the fact that portions of *Ulysses* published in the *Little Review* were on trial for obscenity at the time Joyce was writing the episode. Furthermore, it may not be accidental that Joyce added "print anything now" (U 69.10) to the passage in "Calypso" that Pound had censored because it described Bloom defecating.

Many other late revisions can be read reflexively in the same manner. We are reminded that the book consists of "a few wellchosen words" (U 140.1). Joyce's comment in a letter to Budgen about the extravagance of "Oxen of the Sun" appears as Ned Lambert's response to Dan Dawson's inflated rhetoric: "How's that for high?" (U 123.31–32). We are often advised to steer toward the *Odyssey*, such as when Joyce adds to Mulligan's comment, "Ah, Dedalus, the Greeks": "I must teach you. You must read them in the original" (U 5.7–8). The book's structure is emphasized with the addition of "wheels within wheels" (U 163.7). Two of my chapter titles are late revisions that appear within a page at the end of "Nausicaa"—"Good idea the repetition" (U 377.36); "Life, love, voyage round your own little world" (U 377.2–3). "Wants to stamp his trademark on everything" (U 378.7–8) is added on the next page. Even the passage that provides me with my subtitle and that commemorates the book's publication deadline is a late revision, added after June, 1921, when the

8. Groden, *"Ulysses" in Progress*, 42, 188.

fortieth-birthday target date was known. "Smith O'Brien. Someone has laid a bunch of flowers there. Woman. Must be his deathday. For many happy returns" (U 93.11–13). The fact that 16 June 1904 marks the fortieth anniversary of Smith O'Brien's death only adds to the symmetry.

These and similar revisions make me want to add to Arnold Goldman's claim that "by its fifteenth chapter, *Ulysses* has begun to provide its author enough in the way of material to become self-perpetuating."[9] *Ulysses'* material is not only character, plot, or details of a Dublin setting but also its own language. That language, as part of a language system without beginning or end, allows Joyce continually to create new meanings and formal possibilities for his book. But, in one sense, it is not really Joyce who is creating these meanings or potential forms. They are meanings and forms already available in a language that exists prior to any one reader or writer of that language.

It is in this respect that the structuralists' proclamation of the death of the author and the priority of language over consciousness is useful in talking about *Ulysses*. The language that makes up *Ulysses* has not been injected with some special quality, nor is it the embodiment of its author's consciousness. Instead, it is as Stanley Fish describes all literary language, "language around which we have drawn a frame, a frame that indicates a decision to regard with a particular self-consciousness the resources language has always possessed. . . . What characterizes literature then is not formal properties, but an attitude —always within our power to assume—toward properties that belong by a constitutive right to language."[10]

Fish's view of literary language would indicate that, if we reread any text long enough, it would reflect on itself as language. If so, the question remains, What is special about the language of *Ulysses*? To answer that, I would like to hold out in part for the role of the author. If, as I have argued, Joyce is a reader of language who is open to language's infinite possibilities, chances are good that he will arrange the

9. Arnold Goldman, *The Joyce Paradox* (Evanston: Northwestern University Press, 1968), 99.
10. Stanley Fish, "How Ordinary Is Ordinary Language?" *New Literary History*, V (Autumn, 1973), 52.

words of his text in such a way as to foreground some of those possibilities. Perhaps Victor Shklovsky's term *defamiliarization* would be
helpful here, although what is defamiliarized is language itself.[11] For
Joyce, that process of defamiliarization, which is recorded in the important late revisions, seems to have come in the act of rereading.
Having externalized language by giving it objective existence in a text,
he was free to read it with renewed freshness, rather than as a product of his own consciousness.

Joyce, of course, had the advantage that, since he was the book's
author, he did not have to read with an eye toward the author's intention, theme, moral vision, or even implied consciousness. Instead, he
could concentrate more than could later readers on reading language
on its own terms. As a result, I would like to make an important variation on Georges Poulet's description of the experience of reading.
Poulet tells us that "reading, then, is the act in which the subjective
principle which I call *I*, is modified in such a way that I no longer have
the right, strictly speaking, to consider it as my *I*. I am on loan to another, and this other thinks, feels, suffers, and acts within me." I would
agree that the subject is modified in reading, but what it is on loan to is
not so much "another" as to language itself. In other words, to a large
extent reading retains its passive character, but it is not the case that,
as Schopenhauer claimed, "when we read, someone else thinks for us:
we merely repeat his mental process."[12] Instead, reading is an activity
that can heighten our awareness that it is language that thinks through
us. The reader—that includes its author—is necessary to activate the
language of the text, but is not necessarily in total control over it.

Joyce continually works to make us aware of language. One way
he does so is to make us aware of its materiality. For instance, one
series of late revisions was to alter the spelling of M'Intosh. At first,
macintosh, both cloak and character, was spelled mackintosh. By the
time of the final printing, however, we have macintosh, mackintosh,

---

11. Victor Shklovsky, "Art as Technique," in *Russian Formalist Criticism: Four Essays*, trans. Lee T. Lemon and Marion J. Reis (Lincoln: University of Nebraska Press,
1965), 12.

12. Georges Poulet, "Phenomenology of Reading," *New Literary History*, I (October,
1969), 57; Arthur Schopenhauer, *Schopenhauers Sämtliche Werke in fünf Banden*, ed.
Eduard Grisenbach (5 vols.; Leipzig: Reclam, 1910), V, 291.

and M'Intosh. Such foregrounding of language has led to that wide-spread complaint in *Ulysses* criticism: *Ulysses* has an excess of language. Indeed, this complaint reveals much about critics' attitude toward language. In *Ulysses* we may well have an excess of language, words refusing to be fixed by the traditional form of the novel or any other traditional literary form, an excess that does much more than advance the book's action, since it is also showing what language freed from a purely referential function can do. Confronted with this play of language, several critics try to limit the book, fitting it into preconceived norms, whether aesthetic or moral.

One norm that academic critics frequently impose on *Ulysses*, and one that assures that it will remain human centered, is the generic label of the novel, that product of Western Europe's "liberal imagination." An advantage (and disadvantage) of fitting a work into a certain genre is that we have guidelines for reading it. If someone first reads Swift's *A Modest Proposal* in a class on satire rather than as a pamphlet bought on the streets of eighteenth-century London, certain choices in reading will have been made for him. He knows to look for "irony," a "persona," etc. Similarly, someone reading *Ulysses* as a novel—even if an exceptional someone—knows to look for the humanistic revelation of character brought about in dramatically rendered action.

Even at this point *Ulysses* presents problems because readers are uncertain about which strain of the novel it belongs to. Does it belong to the Irish comic tradition, as Vivian Mercier would have it? The Flaubertian tradition, as Pound and I have read it? Twentieth-century British fiction, as it is most often taught in American universities? Or the tradition of self-conscious fiction, as Robert Alter defines it? Nonetheless, once *Ulysses* has been labeled a novel, a great amount of critical effort is spent trying to uncover the plot that is said to be screened by the language of the book's second half: an effort that can easily distract us from the primary task of concentrating on reading the book's language. As James Maddox says of "Oxen of the Sun": "It is proper to say, then, that we do not so much *read* this chapter as we *translate* it."[13] This is, of course, exactly the point. If a reader tries to translate

13. Maddox, *Joyce's "Ulysses and the Assault upon Character,* 173. Considering the later chapters as translations is widespread; Groden, *"Ulysses" in Progress,* 44, wisely clari-

the chapter into the familiar forms and norms of the novel, he no longer reads the words before him, but replaces them with a text of his own making.

Another attempt to control *Ulysses'* excess of language is, as I pointed out, to dig beneath *Ulysses'* language to try to reveal its underlying theme or moral vision. Whether this theme or vision turns out to be the depravity of the modern world, the integrity of the individual, *caritas*, the classical temper, the relationship between father and son, or incest, the "discovery" of a theme or vision gives the book's language a purpose. It is there to illustrate that theme or vision, and when it does not contribute to that purpose, it is excessive. But even if we overlook the fact that more often than not the moral visions that critics posit are ones they had before reading the book and that their themes are ones that happen personally to interest them, we can see that, rather than admit the limitations of their reading, most critics prefer to reject those parts of the book that do not contribute to elucidating what they have decided it should be doing. Or, when critics do decide to revise their choice of theme or vision to account for all the book's language, their new theme or vision becomes so general and banal that it does not help us in our reading of the book at all.

What the attempts to uncover plot, theme, and vision show is that what we have come to call a reading of the book is in effect a misnomer. To produce a reading is inevitably to limit the possibilities of reading. It turns a process into an object, thus keeping us from reading the book's words with the openness that Joyce did in writing the book.

It is Joyce's openness to language that causes him to foreground its workings. In this sense, what the name Joyce attached to the text means is not so much a person as a way of reading language. If Joyce's name were attached to, say, *Love Story*, we would read its language differently. As Bloom thinks, listening to a piece of music in "Sirens":

---

fies his use of that term. For an account of Joyce as a not so literal translator of his own work, see Jacqueline Risset, "Joyce traduit par Joyce," *Tel Quel*, LV (Autumn, 1973), 47–58. A. Walton Litz, "The Genre of *Ulysses*," in *The Theory of the Novel*, ed. John Halperin (New York: Oxford University Press, 1974), 109–20, makes a compelling argument against forcing *Ulysses* into the extrinsic genre of the novel.

"Know the name you know better" (*U* 278.11–12). It is Joyce's awareness of the potentiality of language that allows us to talk about *Ulysses*
writing itself and that makes *Ulysses* the perfect example of Valéry's
statement that "a work of art is never finished, but only abandoned."
My point is, however, that *Ulysses* has been abandoned only by Joyce,
not by its readers. *Ulysses* will never be finished until it is abandoned
by its readers, for each time that a reader reads and rereads *Ulysses*,
he repeats with a difference the process by which Joyce created the
book.

The reading model I am suggesting, in which the roles of reader
and writer merge, is one that many will resist as too subjective. It
seems to make the language of the text available for the reader to
make over according to his own prejudices. While there is a danger of
subjectivity with this model, it is not as large as some might suppose.
Furthermore, there is an equally strong danger of subjectivity when it
masquerades as objectivity. As I have tried to show, those critics who
claim objectively to have found the underlying theme, moral message,
authorial intention, or even form of *Ulysses* are the ones who more
often than not impose their own norms on the text, since the text, as
Joyce wrote it (and read it) has no inherent norm but is continually
challenging whatever norms we bring to bear upon it. Just as I argued
that an author gains increased "objectivity" not by eliminating his subjectivity but by accounting for it, so, I would argue, does the critic. In
neither case does accounting for subjectivity imply giving it priority,
since pure subjectivity is as false a concept as is pure objectivity. For
example, even though I have called the norms that objectivist critics
impose on *Ulysses* "their" norms, they are really not subjective norms.
They rarely originate with one critic. Instead, they are inherited norms,
norms agreed upon by an entire segment of culture, norms that
through the strength of convention seem to have an ontological status.
It is because the subject is always already constituted by a system
of signs existing prior to him that we can have an interpretive model
that accounts for the reader's response without championing his
subjectivity.

One such model is offered by Walter Benn Michaels in an essay
attacking David Bleich's proposal to substitute the "subjective paradigm" for the worn-out "objective paradigm." As Michaels points out,

Bleich's subjective paradigm is really not that much different from the objective paradigm that he attacks. The objective paradigm, one still defended by critics like M. H. Abrams and E. D. Hirsch, who fear reader-oriented criticism because of what they see as its inherent subjectivity, results from a questionable textual model. This reading model is "the nineteenth-century scientistic model of the autonomus reader or observer confronting an autonomous text or data. If all goes well, the reader suspends his prejudices and interprets the text correctly. If all doesn't go well, the reader enforces his prejudices and makes the text over in their image." Yet Bleich's championing of the subjective paradigm does not really change this model. While Bleich will deny the "autonomy of what is 'out there,'" he continues to hold out for the autonomy of the self. As Michaels sums up, in terms of a textual model, "Bleich's (and Norman Holland's) 'subjectivist' understanding of the self is exactly the same as Abrams' and Hirsch's. The only difference is that Bleich and Holland like what they see and Abrams and Holland don't."[14]

Michaels feels that we need to replace our outdated reading model and model of the interpreter's self with one that he finds implied by C. S. Peirce. "In Peirce's view," he argues, "the self is already embedded in a context, the community of interpretation or system of signs. The rhetoric of the community of interpretation emphasizes the role readers play in constituting texts, while the rhetoric of the self as sign in a system of signs emphasizes the role texts play in constituting consciousness—the strategy in each is to collapse the distinction between the interpreter and what he interprets." The new model, therefore, locates its origin neither in the empty moment before constitution (the "objective paradigm") nor in the reified world after (the "subjective paradigm") but in the act of constitution itself. The point "is not only that reading is constitutive but that readers have themselves been constituted, and hence that the critic's pose of neutrality is as fictitious as the philosopher's."[15]

14. Walter Benn Michaels, "The Interpreter's Self: Peirce on the Cartesian 'Subject,'" *Georgia Review*, XXXI (Summer, 1977), 401.
15. *Ibid.*, 401, 402.

Michaels of course is writing about the controls exerted on the subject in terms of large cultural codes. I would add that there are also controls exerted when one deals with specific texts, like *Ulysses*. Even the most radical exponent of subjective interpretation would agree that when we are interpreting a text we should deal with the words of the text as written. Even when the roles of reader and author merge, no one gives a reader other than Joyce or textual editors the authority to change the words of a text. But the reader's limitation, working with the words as given, actually puts him in a position closer to author Joyce than we might think. Joyce is as aware as any up-to-date semiotician that the words appearing in his texts are part of a sign system existing prior to him. As Stephen complains while talking to the dean of studies in *A Portrait*: "The language in which we are speaking is his before it is mine. . . . His language, so familiar and so foreign, will always be for me an acquired speech. I have not made or accepted its words" (*P* 189). Indeed, when Stephen, the artist, appears in *Ulysses* he is still speaking, thinking, and writing in someone else's language. His most notable sayings are cribbed from Wilde and others, his thoughts are full of quotations, and his attempt at a poem echoes one by Douglas Hyde. In "Telemachus" he has complained, "I am the servant of two masters . . . an English and an Italian" (*U* 20.27–28), which refers as much to his linguistic masters as to his political and religious ones. (In "Aeolus" the professor laments, "We serve them. I teach the blatant Latin language. I speak the tongue of a race the acme of whose mentality is the maxim: time is money" [*U* 133.12–14].) In this respect the forger of his race's conscience is much like his creator, who creates one of the century's most original works by forging together already existing material in inherited languages, for *Ulysses* as we have it results not only from Joyce's rereading of what he has already written but also from Joyce's reading of obituary notices, pubs' ads, speeches, divorce suits, and even other works of literature.

There is, however, a major difference between Joyce and Stephen. Joyce, unlike Stephen, seems to have learned to accept the words he has inherited, an acceptance that allows him, using the technique of *bricolage*, to write *Ulysses* by fitting together already existing myths and historical events and already existing words and phrases. Joyce's creation and transformation of literary forms are less a matter of "natural genius"[16] than an ability to allow language continually to repeat itself with a difference—which could well be a rudimentary description of the act of reading that Joyce has made available to those readers of *Ulysses* willing to repeat (with a difference) the process by which Joyce wrote the book.

What I am implying is not only that the reader of *Ulysses* is conditioned by larger cultural codes prior to approaching *Ulysses* but also that, in reading *Ulysses*, he is being conditioned by the words he reads. That is to say, as others before me have, that *Ulysses* teaches us how to read it as we read. Any longtime reader of *Ulysses* knows that, after a while, he starts to see the world in Ulyssean terms. Thus, the truism seems to follow that he also sees *Ulysses* in Ulyssean terms. It makes much more sense to read *Ulysses* according to the metaphors and interpretive models it provides than to try to base our reading on some external method that promises validity in interpretation. The reader is not distorting the text so long as he sees the text through the text's eyes and I's. The problem is of course that even coming up with the text's interpretive models involves an act of interpretation. It is this continual process, however, that makes the metaphor of the odyssey so appropriate in describing the reading process.

I want to look at one way in which the book instructs the reader as to his role, before I turn to some specific cases of interpretation in the book. Throughout *Ulysses* we are presented with acts of reading and writing. Not surprisingly, these acts comment on the reading and writing of *Ulysses*. As I have argued, we cannot understand one without understanding the other. If we hope to understand the reader's

---

16. It is interesting to look at what precedes "sheer force of natural genius, that" (*U* 646.29). In the text it reads, "However, reverting to the original, there were on the other hand others who had forced their way to the top from the lowest rung by the aid of their bootstraps." In the original manuscript, however, *forged* replaces *forced*. Which word Joyce wanted in this context is problematic. For my purposes, *forged* works better—as a not too subtle reminder that "natural genius" has more to do with creating "genuine forgeries" (*U* 634.25) than with creating originals. Stephen, by the way, has on a pair of borrowed boots. See James Joyce, *Ulysses: The Manuscript and First Printings Compared*, annotated by Clive Driver (New York: Octagon Books, 1975), 601.

role better, a good place to start is the writer's role. Acts of writing imply later acts of reading, although writers themselves were, first, readers. Before returning to acts of reading, I will turn to the acts of writing that produce them.

We have already looked at how Bloom, writing his letter to Martha, reveals his "artistic touch." But we have not remarked upon the fact that Bloom, like his creator, is a prolific letter writer (see the three volumes of Joyce's letters). Molly claims that he wrote her "a letter every morning sometimes twice a day" (U 747.12). He writes letters, real or imagined, to Martha, the ladies of fashion, the *Irish Cyclist*, and the court missionary of the Reformed Priests' Protection Society. That last was "a poem in itself" (U 494.2). We might go so far as to say that, as a character in a work of fiction, Bloom is a man of letters who later in the day loses a letter and temporarily becomes Boom. Perhaps it is not accidental, as Fritz Senn points out, that one of Bloom's first acts of the day is "righting [Molly's] breakfast things on the humpy tray" (U 55.7). Like other forms of writing, Bloom's "righting" is an attempt to place some sort of order on a bit of chaos.

The number of letters that Bloom writes is a reflection not only of Joyce's habits but also of the habits of his fellow Dubliners. It is a commonplace of *Ulysses* criticism to remark that Joyce's Dublin is a town full of great speakers; it is less often noted that it is also a town full of writers. In fact, given the nature of Dublin's talk, which, Hugh Kenner argues, produces "a whole community agreed upon this one thing, that no one at bottom knows what he is talking about because there is nothing to know except talk,"[17] many Dubliners realize that, if you have ambitions to be taken seriously, you have to put in print what you want to say.

When Mr. Deasy wants to make a proposal about foot-and-mouth disease, he writes a letter to the editor. Whether it will be accepted is questionable, because so many other Dubliners know to rely on the power of the pen. When Stephen gives it to A.E. in order to place it in Mr. Norman's journal, A.E. replies, "O, yes. If he considers it important it will go in. We have so much correspondence" (U 192.40–41).

17. Hugh Kenner, *Joyce's Voices* (Berkeley: University of California Press, 1978), 53.

Joyce's Dublin is indeed a city full of letters. In addition to Bloom's and Deasy's letters, there is Rumbold's letter, Blazes' letter to Molly, Milly's to Bloom, Bloom's father's to Leopold, Cunningham's letter to Conmee, Conmee's letter to the father provincial, Stephen's letter to Dolmetsch, the anonymous letter in the Parnell case, the archbishop's letter, and more. Even the narrator of "Cyclops," who has a verbal skill to match Mulligan's, bothered by the growling and growsing of Garryowen, suggests, "Someone that has nothing better to do ought to write a letter *pro bono publico* to the papers about the muzzling order for a dog the like of that" (*U* 311.29–31). Perhaps part of the joke is that, when Joyce puts the narrator's oral rendition of the barroom scenes in print, his wit, if not completely muzzled, is effectively exposed as shallow by Bloom, who despite his lack of eloquence rises in our esteem.

As the case of the narrator in "Cyclops" shows, even Dubliners capable of holding their own in Dublin's battle of verbal wit are aware of the power lodged in the silence of print. Joyce's alter ego, Stephen, who demonstrates his verbal talents to small audiences in both his rendition of the parable of the plums and his Shakespeare theory, knows that the written word makes an impression on more than a piece of paper. Failing to keep his appointment with Buck Mulligan in the Ship to drink up his salary, Stephen sends a telegram. As Stephen had hoped, his printed message provokes a much more appreciative response from Mulligan than if Stephen had appeared in person. Mulligan, that master of Dublin's oral wit, must admit, "Telegram! . . . Wonderful inspiration! Telegram! A papal bull!" (*U* 199.18–19). Since the telegram quotes George Meredith, it seems that Stephen's inspiration lies not in the originality of his message but in the inventiveness of relying on the printed word rather than on the inspired breath of the spoken word to best Mulligan. Similar to his creator, who gave Stephen life through the printed, not spoken, word, Stephen knows that his future talent lies in exercising his penmanship, not his voice. Listening to Professor MacHugh re-create John F. Taylor's impromptu speech delivered without notes in the windy chapter of "Aeolus," Stephen thinks, "Noble words coming. Look out. Could you try your hand at it yourself?" (*U* 142.14–15). Hand, not voice.

What the Dubliners realize is the advantage of having words fixed to a page. A writer does not have to worry that his words, like the orator's, will be "gone with the wind" (*U* 143.28). Recorded on a piece of paper, a writer's words may well outlive him. The existence of a text also allows the reader freedoms that a listener doesn't have with spoken words. If he wants, a reader can store a text away (in a drawer or side pocket perhaps) and read it when he is in the mood, a possibility that allows him to read a text (as Bloom does) more than once. He can scrutinize and study it and allow his mind to fantasize a variety of interpretations.

Nonetheless, the reader's freedom creates a problem for the writer. What may sound original and witty if heard once, sounds worn out and clichéd if read a number of times. Given the text of a speech, even a good one, a reader can offer a much more exacting critique. This is doubly true for a bad speech. The point is made very clearly in that chapter of *Ulysses* that shows the process by which the spoken word is turned from breath to print. In "Aeolus" a group of Dubliners gathered in the newspaper office tears apart the inflated rhetoric of Dan Dawson. Bloom, however, is more sympathetic. Harboring secret desires to be a powerful speaker himself, he knows that with a live audience Dawson's rhetoric is quite effective. "All very fine to jeer at it now in cold print but it goes down like hot cake that stuff" (*U* 126.15–16).

It is also Bloom in the chapter preceding "Aeolus" who contemplates a problem that must have plagued Joyce while writing *Ulysses* in self-imposed exile from Dublin. Surrounded by the graves of the silent dead in "Hades," Bloom ponders how to keep the memory of the dead alive.

How many! All these here once walked round Dublin. Faithful departed. As you are now so once were we.

Besides how could you remember everybody? Eyes, walk, voice. Well, the voice, yes: gramophone. Have a gramophone in every grave or keep it in the house. After dinner on a Sunday. Put on poor old greatgrandfather Kraahraark! Hellohellohello amawfullyglad kraark awfullygladaseeragain hellohello amarawf kopthsth. Remind you of the voice like the photograph reminds you of the face. Otherwise you couldn't remember the face after fifteen years, say. For instance who? For instance some fellow that died when I was in Wisdom Hely's.

Rtststr! A rattle of pebbles. Wait. Stop. (*U* 113.41–114.10)

Appropriate to a chapter introducing the themes of death and resurrection, Bloom's musings unwittingly comment on Joyce's effort to resurrect a living Dublin and all its voices out of the silence of the past with nothing more than the ghostly graveyard of memory and the silence of print. As Bloom thinks later in the day, "Want a good memory" (*U* 272.30). But human memory, Bloom reminds us in his passage, is fallible. As if to illustrate his point, Bloom, just before his thoughts about Dublin's dead, confuses Zeuxis, who painted a picture of grapes so realistic that he even confused birds, with Apollo via Apelles. "The Sacred Heart that is: showing it. Heart on his sleeve. Ought to be sideways and red it should be painted like a real heart. Ireland was dedicated to it or whatever that. Seems anything but pleased. Why this infliction? Would birds come then and peck like the boy with the basket of fruit but he said no because they ought to have been afraid of the boy. Apollo that was" (*U* 113.34–40).

The allusion to Zeuxis' painting, along with Bloom's own insistence on realistic representation, reminds us of another problem that writing *Ulysses* raised for Joyce. Joyce not only wanted to resurrect the past, he wanted to resurrect it with the realistic accuracy of Zeuxis. He suffered from the "infliction" to want to make the "that was" as vivid as the "that is." Practical Bloom offers one solution for a writer intent on accurately recording the voices of the dead—a gramophone. But Joyce did not have the foresight to place a number of gramophones around Dublin, 16 June 1904, to record the voices of all the great talkers he wanted to include in *Ulysses*. Even more important, Joyce could no more compose *Ulysses* with a gramophone than he could with a collection of photographs. For a writer demanding strict realism, the problem of accurately recording a voice in print presents no easy solution.

An important assumption of realism is that an artist can find a transparent medium that does not intrude upon the representation of reality. But realism is impossible because the artist's medium intrudes, interfering with our suspension of disbelief. Because *Ulysses* is made up of "signs on a white field" (U 48.24–25) and because those signs are decidedly silent, Joyce cannot merely record the sounds of an already existing Dublin. Instead Joyce's Dublin is a world created with words, and those words more than anything else dictate the nature of the world he presents. Joyce's medium of written language will always interfere in any attempt to record the voices and sounds of Dublin, just as in Bloom's imagined use of the gramophone the medium interferes with the direct recording of the voice and calls attention to itself. "Kraahraark!" It is not surprising that, in trying to record the gramophone's interference, Joyce must invent a "word" that calls attention to his own printed medium. Indeed the "words" making up the passage recording the recording of the gramophone—a recording that exists in Bloom's imagination—resemble, more than anything, the words of *Finnegans Wake*, a book that makes intrusions of the medium more obvious. But we need not turn to *Finnegans Wake* to find such overt intrusions of the medium. In *Ulysses* even Stephen's notion of God as the immediacy of a noise in the street is mocked in "Circe" when the noise in the street occurs through the medium of a gramophone playing "The Holy City." The gramophone ends up producing not God's voice and not even music, but the rasping noise of a needle grating a disc. This interfering noise of the medium in turn drowns out the voice of Elijah proclaiming his revelation. Revelation in *Ulysses* is always mediated.

In *Ulysses*, Joyce's medium more and more comes to the foreground. More and more we become aware that, rather than being passively recorded, the voices of Dublin exist because of the rhetorical powers of the written language. Rhetoric, rather than placing a screen between us and realistic representation, is a necessary component of realism. But for us once again to be made aware of the connection between rhetoric and realism, Joyce first had to abandon all pretensions to realism and unveil the previously disguised workings of rhetoric. And in calling attention to the workings of rhetoric, Joyce also calls attention to himself as a manipulator of language. It is Joyce, the master ventriloquist, who gives voice to all the characters of *Ulysses*. Thus, in setting out to record the immediacy of Dublin's voices, Joyce introduces a new "voice" into the world of *Ulysses*—his own.

So Bloom's musings in the graveyard raise still another question that must have plagued Joyce as he dedicated his life to creating a work of fiction. How could he make certain that his own voice could be remembered, for in addition to attempting to resurrect the voices of a past Dublin for the present, *Ulysses* is also a vehicle by which Joyce could try to keep his own voice alive for the future. The task is not an easy one because the present soon becomes the past, and Joyce's voice, like those in the cemetery, is doomed to become a silent one. "As you are now so once were we" (*U* 113.42). How, then, is Joyce to keep his voice alive to speak to the future, which is the sister of the past?

As much as the two problems raised by Bloom—the resurrection of past voices for the present and the keeping alive of Joyce's present voice for the future—seem related, they could be seen as leading to two different theories about the nature of fiction and the role of the author. The resurrection of the past for the present can lead to the notion that fiction is realistic and objective. The role of the author in such a theory is to be a passive medium through which the sounds and voices, among other things, of a living Dublin are recorded in a text. On the other hand, the notion that *Ulysses* keeps alive Joyce's voice seems to assume just the opposite. No longer does the author exist as a passive medium through which the voices of Dublin are kept alive. Now, the text becomes the medium by which the author's voice is kept alive. *Ulysses* is no longer an objective record of Dublin, but can now be seen as Joyce's subjective creation—a product of his imagination. Although it has proclaimed its exile from Dublin, Joyce's voice seems doomed to intrude in any attempt to represent Dublin in literature. Thus, the objective notion of fiction and the subjective notion of fiction merge at the very instant that representation is attempted. In order to keep the voices of Dublin alive, Joyce must keep his own voice alive. But his voice is worth keeping alive because of the skill with which he can create voices other than his own.

With all this emphasis on keeping the voices of Dublin's faithful departed alive, Bloom's simple question remains, If not with a gramophone, how? If Joseph Conrad claims that his task as novelist is, through the power of the written word, to make us "see," we might say that Joyce's task is, despite the silence of the written word, to make us "hear." But how can we hear the voices of Dublin when we silently read? Or, to pose a similar question, how can Joyce "speak" to us through his text when what we call his voice is, as I have tried to show, a product of his uncompromisingly silent medium?

In this respect, it is helpful to see *Ulysses* as a continual interaction between two Joyces: Joyce the singer, with an ear sensitive to the sounds that could be recorded on Bloom's gramophone, and Joyce the writer, with his acute awareness that he must record those sounds in a silent medium. These two Joyces are not necessarily in opposition. Certainly, one of the strengths of Joyce the writer is his musician's ear for detecting variations in the minutest of sounds. In fact, Joyce, who once contemplated a career as a singer, late in his life lamented to Sylvia Beach that perhaps he should have cultivated his voice rather than his writing. But instead, having early in his life abandoned his career as a singer for that of a writer, Joyce was forced to learn how to sing the song of himself in silence.

Because written and printed words are silent, to "speak" of a voice in a text is to speak metaphorically. While the voice we encounter in a text has enough in common with a spoken voice to make the term useful, it is important to remember that a textual voice is not a spoken voice, nor is it merely a substitute for a spoken voice. As Dorrit Cohn emphasizes, one of Joyce's major achievements in *Ulysses* is to break with the speech-minus-sound concept of verbal thought. The voice that we hear while reading a text has much more in common with "inner speech," man's capacity to think words rather than utter them.[18] In fact, a quick look at an English dictionary is enough to remind us that even in nonliterary areas *voice* need not refer to actual sounds, just as *record*, which originally referred to a written document, now can refer to something that can produce sound when played on a gramophone. Perhaps the most appropriate definition for the voices we find in texts is the one that refers to a voice as "the agency or means by which something is expressed, represented, or

18. Dorrit Cohn, *Transparent Minds* (Princeton: Princeton University Press, 1978), 93. See Cohn's discussion (95–97) of Lev Vygotsky's psycholinguistic account of the development of this faculty in children.

revealed." The way in which that something is expressed, represented, or revealed in writing brings us back to the role of the reader. There is an important difference between a spoken and a written voice: the manner in which they are perceived.

A listener can remain relatively passive and still hear a spoken voice, but a written voice can only be heard through the *activity* of reading. (Thus we feel that reading improves our children's minds by making them actively create a voice and picture from the text, while television deadens their minds by letting them passively receive voice and picture.) Indeed, it is the reader who gives substance to the metaphor of a textual voice. On the one hand, the reader is like the blind stripling Bloom encounters, who, because he cannot see Dublin, gets his sense of its reality from the sounds he hears. "Would he feel it if something was removed? Feel a gap. Queer idea of Dublin he must have, tapping his way round by the stones" (*U* 181.27–29). He recognizes Bloom as a man because of his voice. "Knows I'm a man. Voice" (*U* 181.20). On the other hand, the reader is confronted with a silent text in which "the voices blend and fuse in clouded silence" (*U* 414.3). The reader's task is to unsilence these voices, to make them heard again.

Before the act of reading, the voices of *Ulysses* remain embalmed in the "mummery of their letters" (*U* 28.12). But when the reader reads those silent letters, he releases the voices of *Ulysses* from the mummery of print and allows them to speak again. Rather than thinking of all the voices of Dublin, including its author's, as contained in *Ulysses*, we might think of those voices existing only when they are freed from the text by the act of reading. Without the reader, an author remains silent and abandoned, a ghost by death or absence. With the reader, the author's voice is given breath and the spirit is resurrected to speak continually to new generations of readers. Or, to apply another favorite metaphor of Joyce's, the reader inherits the author's voice just as a son inherits his father's voice. The voice of the father-author lives when heard by the son-reader.

It is exactly the necessity of a voice to be recognized that Joyce stresses in *Ulysses*, and it is the exiled father, Kevin Egan, wanting to be remembered to his son, who acknowledges the importance of recognition. As he tells Stephen, "You're your father's son. I know the voice" (*U* 43.10). It is also son Bloom who remembers his father remembering the scene in *Deborah* in which old blind Abraham recognizes his son. "Nathan's voice! His son's voice! I hear the voice of Nathan who left his father to die of grief and misery in my arms, who left the house of his father and left the God of his father" (*U* 76.33–35). Surrogate father Bloom, who is himself sonless, referring to Stephen's musical talents, admits that "he more than suspected he had his father's voice" (*U* 659.2). Even Stephen thinks of his father as "the man with my voice" (*U* 38.11). Finally, it is important to remember that Stephen's interpretation of *Hamlet* depends upon his giving an identity to the ghost of a father speaking to a son, "a voice heard only in the heart of him who is the substance of his shadow, the son consubstantial with the father" (*U* 197.14–15). That ghost, according to Stephen, is the author Shakespeare returning to the play he has created, staying alive by pleading with audience and son, "Remember me."

In *Ulysses*, Joyce has indeed given us the ghost story the children in "Nestor" ask for, just as Stephen turns *Hamlet* into one. "He will have it that *Hamlet* is a ghoststory" (*U* 187.39). As a writer, he breathes life into almost forgotten figures and resurrects them as living characters. "Let there be life" (*U* 145.10), Stephen remarks as he is about to tell his parable of the plums. Then in "Oxen of the Sun," Stephen adds, "You have spoken of the past and its phantoms. . . . Why think of them? If I call them into life across the waters of Lethe will not the poor ghosts troop to my call? Who supposes it? I, Bous Stephanoumenos, bullockbefriending bard, am lord and giver of their life" (*U* 415.3–7). Odysseus descended into Hades and allowed the shades to speak by feeding them blood. Joyce allows dead voices to speak again by feeding them the blood of language.

But once that language is committed to print, Joyce himself becomes the ghost and will be doomed to silent exile unless attentive readers detect his voice haunting the world of Dublin he has created. Because Joyce is a writer of novels, not plays, he even more than Shakespeare runs the risk of having his voice remain in silence. As a writer, he cannot return to the stage to plead with us that he be remembered. Instead he must lose his voice to the silence of print in order to save it. Thus, Joyce becomes much like Stephen, who, in refusing to sing in "Circe," proclaims, "No voice. I am a most finished artist" (*U* 518.13). Without a voice, a writer is indeed finished—dead—and yet, as a finished—refined—artist, Joyce learned to adopt techniques of cunning to ensure that his voice would stay alive.

In fact, reading Joyce's works in retrospective arrangement, we can place Stephen's vow of silence, exile, and cunning, as he is about to embark on a career of writing, in a new context. Silence is the silence forced upon him by his medium of print. Exile is the exile that every writer faces once he commits his work to print and can no longer be a presence within it. And cunning is the cunning Joyce needed to keep his voice alive despite his silent exile from the text.

The reader's task of giving voice to the silent words of print is not an easy one. One of the paradoxes of language in print is that, although words may be fixed to a page, they do not yield fixed meanings. Instead they can be read many ways and produce many voices. I have already emphasized the rabbit-duck-like comments that can be read as part of both the naturalistic tale and the tale of the telling. Appropriately, when read as part of the tale of the telling, these comments instruct us on our role in reading the book. To review, many phrases can be read as exposing the book as a linguistic counterfeit, others as comments on Joyce's writing of the book, and still others on his use of the *Odyssey*. We are also advised to read in retrospective arrangement and with agility and training of the eye. One of the most explicit comments on how to read the book occurs as Bloom watches the typesetter in "Aeolus": "Reads it backwards first. Quickly he does it. Must require some practice that" (*U* 122.18–19). Soon after, we read, "Sounds a bit silly till you come to look into it well" (*U* 122.28). If we do come to look into *Ulysses* well, we can better appreciate Myles Crawford's instructions to Stephen to "put us all into it, damn its soul. Father Son and Holy Ghost an Jakes M'Carthy" (*U* 135.23–24). We can also read Bloom's thoughts about Stephen's father in a different context. "It's the droll way he comes out with the things. Knows how to tell a story too" (*U* 152.25–26). Indeed in *Ulysses* we can agree with Bloom. "See? it all works out" (*U* 154.19–20).

In addition to comments on the entire book, *Ulysses* includes comments on individual chapters. In the musical performance of "Sirens" we hear, "If he doesn't conduct himself I'll wring his ear for him a yard long" (U 258.28–29). "Eumaeus" is labeled the "circumlocution departments" (U 627.27), and, in "Circe," Stephen unknowingly alerts us to the chapter's title by mistaking Circe for Ceres (U 504.4–5).

More important than providing these sly comments, the tale of the telling foregrounds different aspects of language in different chapters. Having been alerted to one quality of language in one chapter, we can reread the words of other chapters with this quality in mind. This type of rereading, as much as anything, produces the book's mirror-within-a-mirror effect. I have already shown how the tropological nature of names that we find in "Eumaeus" is reflected throughout the book. Similarly, in "Aeolus," Joyce gives us language arranged as if it occurred in a newspaper. As Carol Shloss points out, the chapter's style gives us a way of thinking about the technique of the entire book. Quoting Joyce on his comment that "each adventure . . . should not only condition but even create its own technique" (Letters, I 147), she asks, "What is the result of this methodology if not the corporate language of a newspaper with its women's pages, advice to the lovelorn, sports talk, and political analyses? We have assumed for years that there is a language appropriate to the ladies, to the jocks, to the lawyers of the community, and that items of interest to each audience should 'not only condition but even create [their] own technique.'"[19]

If "Aeolus" invites us to think of the book as a newspaper, "Circe" invites us to think of it in terms of drama. Thus, Fritz Senn has been able to point out how, in the first chapter, adverbs are used like stage directions, helping create the sense of role playing. In another chapter, "Sirens," we are alerted to the sound of words, very often through truncated words. But truncated words occur outside "Sirens," although at first we might not pay attention to their sounds. In "Calypso": "The sweated legend in the crown of his hat told [Bloom] mutely: Plasto's high grade ha" (U 56.39–40). As the book progresses, however, that ha starts to be increasingly heard. On the first

19. Carol Shloss, "Choice Newseryreels: James Joyce and the Irish Times," James Joyce Quarterly, XV (Summer, 1978), 334–35.

page of "Lotus Eaters" we read: "Under their dropped lids his eyes found the tiny bow of the leather headband inside his high grade ha" (*U* 71.28–30). If we are concerned, as some critics are, with locating this sentence in a consciousness, we might ask whether the *ha* signals a movement from objective description into Bloom's mind or whether this is an early example of the book's linguistic play. If the sentence had occurred in "Sirens," in which the language of flowers of "Lotus Eaters" has become the "language of flow" (*U* 263.35–36), we would be fairly sure. But if we notice the *ha* in "Lotus Eaters" only in retrospective arrangement, we are to be excused. Joyce did too. The *ha* for *hat* is a late revision.

Whenever we have to give voice to mute letters on a page or even on a sweated legend in a hat crown, we are involved in an act of interpretation. Should *flow* in the "language of flow" be read as a truncated version of *flowers* rhyming with now or as a complete word rhyming with no? To cite an example early in the book: critics have long assumed that Stephen has paid the rent for the tower because he thinks, "He [Mulligan] wants that key. It is mine, I paid the rent. Now I eat his salt bread. Give him the key too. All. He will ask for it. That was in his eyes" (*U* 20.19–21). But the sentence, "It is mine, I paid the rent," might be Stephen echoing what Mulligan has previously told him. The phrase may be Mulligan's, not Stephen's. Whether Mulligan or Stephen has paid the rent depends on how we give voice to this "key" sentence.[20]

The pages of *Ulysses* are full of models suggesting how to interpret such passages. What these models offer is not a method by which we can be sure of hearing one correct voice but a lesson on how to tune our ears so as to hear many voices, just as Joyce did as he wrote, reread, and rewrote the book. Furthermore, these models imply that, just as Joyce's voice mixes with any attempt to resurrect the voices of Dublin, so the reader's voice mixes with his attempt to resurrect the voices of *Ulysses*. There are some conclusions to be drawn about what these models imply, as we repeat with a difference Joyce's act of reading and rereading the words of *Ulysses*.

20. Hugh Kenner, *Ulysses* (London: George Allen & Unwin, 1980), 54–55, reads the passage in this way and cites Arnold Goldman. Independently of Kenner and Goldman, Fritz Senn suggested this reading to me in conversation.

Chapter Six

It's in the Silence You Feel You Hear

Because *Ulysses* offers so many voices to hear, we cannot simultaneously hear them all. What this means is that any one reading of *Ulysses* is by necessity a partial reading. I mean that in both senses of the word. The inevitability of partiality allows me to risk formulating a principle that applies to any reading of *Ulysses*: every reader makes mistakes. But one of the pleasures of reading the book is that, even for those of us lacking genius, errors can turn into portals of discovery. Mistakes, in fact, have been woven into the fabric of the text.

Look, for instance, as many critics have, at Joyce's carefully planted verbal "mistakes," such as Martha's misspelling of *world* for *word* in her letter to Bloom and the newspaper's misprint of *L. Boom* for *L. Bloom*.[1] In a conventional novel we might pass over the misprints by blaming them on the printer. But Joyce will not let us ignore a "misprint" because a misprint as written generates meaning in the context of the book as a whole. Martha's misspelling connects with Stephen's encounter with his mother's ghost in "Circe":

> STEPHEN
> (*Eagerly.*) Tell me the word, mother, if you know now. The word known to all men. . . .
> THE MOTHER
> I pray for you in my other world. (*U* 581.4–6, 15–16)

The newspaper misprint reminds us that God is a noise in the street.

1. Fritz Senn, "Book of Many Turns," *James Joyce Quarterly*, X (Fall, 1972), 43–44.

In other words, if the mistake is caused by Joyce rather than by an inattentive proofreader (in which case it would become a "real" mistake?), it becomes an economical way to convey information. Not only do we read the mistake, we also "read" the correct word or phrase. We read both what is there and what is not, although, as we saw in the case of M'Intosh, when we read what is not there we inevitably run the risk of error. Indeed, it is mistakes, which introduce the possibility of error, that allow us to read more into *Ulysses* than what is on the page before us—what literally are, after all, merely marks of black ink. As Stephen says, "You find my words dark" (*U* 48.31).

Having proclaimed a reading principle based on error, I want to caution us as to how we take that principle, since a growing number of critics seems to have mis-taken it. There is an increasing consensus in *Ulysses* criticism that *Ulysses* dramatizes the incertitude and possibility of error involved in bringing interpretive models to bear on reality. But advocates of this position too often fail to recognize that, when we designate the perils of interpretation as a theme of the book, we employ exactly the interpretive processes that *Ulysses* continually shows to result in error. In other words, if we claim that *Ulysses* is an attack on all attempts to organize the world in a meaningful manner, we are brought face to face with the fact that we base the insight on a work of fiction. Any insight that we have, even the insight into our own blindness and propensity to error, is undercut. A world founded on error is not a stable one; we cannot be too certain about incertitude.

What I want to emphasize is that, when we isolate the inevitability of error or incertitude as a reading principle, we run the risk of turning that principle into a new critical dogma. Marilyn French, in *The Book as World*, is adamant in insisting that *Ulysses* and our reading of it are founded on the void of incertitude. "By building incertitude into the method of the novel, Joyce places the reader in the same dilemma as the characters. . . . He insists that the reader experience relativity while reading about it." But she goes on to contradict her insight by reifying uncertainty itself. One sentence embodies the contradiction in her method. "Since the theme of the book is the incertitude implicit in the human condition, and since everything in the novel is wound up tightly with this theme, Joyce's point should be clear."[2] Can French be sure of this?

What her notion of the reading process of *Ulysses* makes clear to me is that she has not fully understood the implications of founding a work on the void of incertitude. In her chapter "The Reader and the Journey," she wisely relies on Joyce's own metaphor and claims that the reader is the Ulysses of the title and that his journey through the book is his odyssey. The problem with her notion of the journey is that it is finite. The reader experiences the odyssey of reading the book, only to return to the "rock of Ithaca," where the motion stops. In describing the reader's journey through *Ulysses* as one with a beginning, middle, and end, French can posit the book's initial style as the book's norm, the middle styles as a deviation from the norm, and the end as a return home. As the description of a first reading, this is fine. But *Ulysses* is often read from back to front as well as front to back. In rereading, we can easily posit one of the middle chapters as the book's stylistic norm—"Oxen of the Sun," for instance, whose many styles mirror the effect of the entire book. Because the reader's journey is potentially endless, the book has no established norm, and the reader's journey is potentially endless because the book lacks a normative center. We might remember that when the motion of Shakespeare's odyssey ends, he dies (*U* 213.4).

French's reader can enjoy the luxury of a finite voyage through *Ulysses* because, despite arguing for a limited notion of man, French posits a superreader in total control of the language he confronts. Even though the reader is supposed to be facing uncertainty, we are assured that "the reader is the only person who sees it all, who is aware of all elements inside the novel as well as all things outside to which it alludes." The omniscient author has been replaced by the omniscient reader. "The journey taken in *Ulysses* is the book itself, and only the reader traverses it entirely."[3]

French's reader sounds much like what James H. Maddox calls the

2. Marilyn French, *The Book as World* (Cambridge: Harvard University Press, 1976), 4, 52.
3. *Ibid.*, 4.

book's "ideal first time reader,"[4] although to his credit Maddox admits that such a reader probably does not exist. He cannot exist because of the nature of the act of reading. The reader cannot "see it all": while *Ulysses* may *allow* alternative readings, it does not necessarily *contain* them in the sense that a forest contains trees. *Ulysses* does not contain readings; it contains words. To be sure, by arranging those words in a variety of patterns we produce a reading, but that pattern only comes into existence when someone recognizes its potential through the act of reading, much in the way that Joyce recognized the potential of recycling the *Odyssey* through one day in Dublin. In fact, the word *pattern*—or its counterpart, *mosaic*—is misleading because of its spatial implications. While Joseph Frank is certainly helpful in pointing out the "spatial" character of a work like *Ulysses*, the term remains helpful only so long as we remember its distortions. No matter how many details and phrases we store in our memory later to arrange into a pattern, that arrangement is always sequential. Reading remains a temporal activity. Producing one pattern rules out, for that moment, producing another. We can no more perceive all the alternative readings in our mind at the same time than—to use a visual example that does seem applicable in this particular case—we can simultaneously see both rabbit and duck of the famous gestalt figure. To produce one pattern we have to go through an act of reading, and to produce another pattern we need to go through another act of reading, creating an endless number of structures.

Instead of offering French's reader who traverses the book entirely or Maddox's "ideal first time reader," *Ulysses* provides us with a model of a more limited reader: Molly. If Bloom has a touch of the artist about him, Molly could be said to have a touch of the reader about her. The first time we see her she is reading. We can also assume that sometime shortly after the end of the novel she will resume her reading of *Sweets of Sin*, a work of fiction that will make her reflect on her own adulterous life in another work of fiction—*Ulysses*. So, while Stephen and Bloom have visions of becoming writers,

4. James H. Maddox, *Joyce's "Ulysses" and the Assault upon Character* (New Brunswick: Rutgers University Press, 1978), 207.

and in fact are shown to write during the course of the day, Molly seems to be fairly content with her role as reader. In "Penelope" she thinks longingly of receiving letters. And even if not an ideal or super-reader, she is a fairly sophisticated reader of love letters. She has enough sense to know that love letters cannot be taken literally, that too many "silly women believe love is sighing I am dying" (U 758.32–33). On the other hand, she is not a pure skeptic. She knows that the counterfeit rhetoric of a love letter may contain some truth. For instance, if Blazes would write her a love letter she would "suppose thered be some truth in it true or no it fills up your whole day and life always something to think about every moment and see it all around you like a new world" (U 758.33–36). In other words, as a reader, Molly comes close to us in our desire to believe in what happens in Ulysses, to imagine it like a new world that can fill up our days, despite the fact that at times we don't really know what is happening. And while we can never be sure, we can even imagine that Joyce gave Molly the type of reader's response that he hoped Nora would have when he presented her with Ulysses, that strange love letter written in her honor, which, fortunately or unfortunately, she could not finish.

What we do know is that Joyce uses the same technique to guide his readers as Bloom does to remedy his wife's state of comparative ignorance. Direct instruction had proved useless: "She followed not at all, a part of the whole, gave attention with interest, comprehended with surprise, with care repeated, with greater difficulty remembered, forgot with ease, with misgiving reremembered, rerepeated with error" (U 687.8–11). As readers, we are all Mollys, inevitably failing to understand the whole. Therefore, artist Bloom and artist Joyce adopt a technique of suggestion that personally involves the reader.

What system had proved more effective?
Indirect suggestion implicating self-interest. (U 687.12–13)[5]

The mystery of Molly herself, we find, depends on artist Bloom's using a similar method to elucidate the sign by which she is denoted.

5. Wolfgang Iser, The Implied Reader (Baltimore: Johns Hopkins University Press, 1974), 233, uses the same example.

How did he elucidate the mystery of an invisible person, his wife Marion (Molly) Bloom, denoted by a visible splendid sign, a lamp?

With indirect and direct verbal allusions or affirmations: with subdued affection and admiration: with description: with impediment: with suggestion.

(*U* 702.24–29)

Of course the technique of suggestion lays open the possibility of misreadings, but misreadings are the stuff the book is made of. In fact, it is Molly's ability to allow contradictory interpretations to exist simultaneously that makes her a better reader than she herself might acknowledge.

For instance, confronted with "unusual polysyllables of foreign origin" (*U* 686.30), Molly interprets them phonetically or by false analogy or by both. When she applies her method of misinterpretation to the word *alias*, she not only gives us a comedy of errors but she also helps us understand how Joyce uses names in *Ulysses*. *Alias* she construes as "a mendacious person mentioned in sacred Scripture" (*U* 686.32–33). According to Gifford and Seidman, she confuses the word with "Ananias," a figure in the Bible who, after lying to Peter, drops dead.[6] If this interpretation of her confusion is correct, Molly turns out to be right after all: Ananias has become a colloquialism for liar and an alias is a false name. Gifford and Seidman's identification, while not a mistake, is, however, misleading. By suggesting that there is only one name that Molly confuses, they limit the possible play of Molly's mistake. (Similarly, in glossing the meaning of Stephen's name, they list only Saint Stephen. Certainly, that is not wrong, but we should not be led to believe that he is the only Stephen that Stephen's name suggests.) In fact, it is very likely that at least one other name from the Bible contributes to the play of Molly's confusion—Elias, whose one-letter difference from alias reminds us of the mistake of Boom for Bloom. That the alias for *alias* could be Elias who turns out to be Ananias reminds us of the play of names throughout *Ulysses*, a book masquerading as "sacred scripture" and giving aliases to most of its major characters.

The fact that misinterpretations by characters turn into portals of

6. Don Gifford and Robert J. Seidman, *Notes for Joyce* (New York: E. P. Dutton, 1974), 472.

discovery shows a change in Joyce's attitude from his earlier works to *Ulysses*. In *Dubliners*, when a character misinterprets a scene or another character, the result is paralysis approaching death. The failure of Mr. Duffy and Mrs. Sinico or Gabriel and Gretta to communicate are prime examples of how Joyce uses a "scrupulous meanness" to expose his characters' blindness. In *A Portrait* the tone cuts both ways. When Stephen misinterprets a scene, as he always does, we both appreciate his imagination and laugh at his folly. By *Ulysses*, however, the comic spirit reigns. All the characters make mistakes, but because as readers we make even more mistakes we should no longer feel superior. The reader who feels superior is like Comyn in Stephen's history class. He thinks he knows the correct answer, but finally it is the "ignorant" Armstrong who, through his "mistaken" definition of *pier*, gives Stephen the phrase he needs to formulate his theory of history as "a disappointed bridge" (*U* 25.4), something that Comyn cannot comprehend. There is no one correct reading, so the only totally incorrect reading is the one that claims to be the correct reading.

The Armstrongs of *Ulysses* criticism are the Cyclopean readers who have not developed the agility and training of the eye to read a reflexive book very flexibly. The examples of interpretation we find in *Ulysses* encourage us to pay attention to words rather than to authorial intention. We can even argue that *Ulysses*' author intended it that way. The "foolish author of a wise book" was not one to claim ultimate authority over the words he used. Arthur Power reports the following conversation with Joyce:

> Then in your opinion, I said, the critics and the intellectuals have boggled the issue, have not seen your intention clearly, and have put meanings into it which did not exist, which they have invented for themselves.
>
> Yes and no, replied Joyce shrugging his shoulders evasively, for who knows but it is they who are right. What do we know about what we put into anything? Though people may read more into *Ulysses* than I ever intended, who is to say that they are wrong: do any of us know what we are creating?[7]

The text Joyce created offers a humorous lesson about authorial

---

7. Arthur Power, *Conversations with James Joyce*, ed. Clive Hart (New York: Barnes & Noble, 1974), 89.

intention. It occurs in "Lotus Eaters" when Bantam Lyons "misinterprets" Bloom's remark that he is going to throw away his newspaper. Lyons' initial response seems to indicate that he trusts language too much, causing him to be an overingenious interpreter of language, ignoring authorial intention. Because he is preoccupied with subjective thoughts of the Gold Cup, Lyons immediately makes a connection between Bloom's random statement and a horse race. A skeptic would argue that the connection, not intended by Bloom, is verbal rather than "real." The name of a horse and the verb *throw away* are coincidentally related because of a word and Lyons' overactive mind. Nonetheless, later in the day, when Lyons abandons his faith in Bloom's "tip," he finds himself poorer for it. Thus, despite the fact that Lyons "misreads" Bloom's "tip," linguistic coincidence seems to have a mysterious power of prophecy.

Of course it could be argued that *throw away* is not a coincidence at all, that it was intended and planned by the hidden hand of our arranger.[8] The point I am interested in, however, is what happens to our view of language when time and time again the reader of *Ulysses* is shown linguistic coincidence leading to "meaningful" coincidence. Lyons' giving meaning to a linguistic coincidence is reminiscent of the experience that so many readers of *Ulysses* have when, *Word Index*, *Skeat's*, and *OED* in hand, they start to trace a string of linguistic clues. As more and more "coincidences" start to create a pattern of meaning, the reader finds it impossible to believe that Joyce could have "intended" all the connections he finds. Indeed Joyce may not have intended every one of the connections. The connections may be the result of a system of signs that is prior to any *one* user of those signs. But does that make the coincidences illegitimate in the context created by *Ulysses*? Does not *Ulysses* encourage us to use our ingenuity to read what the play of language might reveal to us?

The most obvious case in which interpretive ingenuity and play are on display in *Ulysses* is Stephen's performance in the library. I would like to return to it now not to examine its content but to see what it

---

8. The useful term *arranger* is David Hayman's in *"Ulysses": The Mechanics of Meaning* (Englewood Cliffs, N.J.: Prentice-Hall, 1970), 70.

implies about the act of interpretation, for at the same time that Stephen gives us a theory about the role of the artist, he dramatizes a role the interpreter might play. Just as Stephen's theory accounts for the subject in the creation of a work of art, so Joyce's dramatization of Stephen working out that theory accounts for the subject in the act of interpretation. While the chapter does not prescribe a method, it does present one example of what happens when understanding takes place as the result of an encounter with a text. From it we can increase our understanding about what occurs in any act of understanding, although to demonstrate that Stephen has indeed achieved a measure of understanding in the chapter, I will have to steer a path between the Scylla and Charybdis of objectivity and subjectivity.

Complaints that Stephen's theory is subjective are easy to understand. As I have already argued, in the first three chapters Stephen appears to be the embodiment of subjectivity. His Shakespeare theory does not seem to escape its dangers. Ostensibly putting forth Stephen's interpretation of how Shakespeare's life interacts with his art, Stephen's theory reveals as much about Stephen the critic as about Shakespeare the artist. Stephen claims that the artist always creates characters in his own image. Similarly, the characters in Stephen's drama resemble their creator. The Shakespeare whom Stephen gives us has remarkable similarities to the Stephen we know. His Stratford becomes Stephen's Dublin; his London, Stephen's Paris. Even Shakespeare's flight to the world of art in London parallels Stephen's flight to the world of art in Paris. Although at the end of A Portrait, Stephen glorifies his escape, it can be interpreted as a way of hiding himself from his rejection by E.C., just as Shakespeare escapes from his relationship with Ann. Stephen's Shakespeare, like Stephen, fears betrayal from those close to him and worries about paternity and fatherhood. Revenge becomes a prime motive in Shakespeare's plays just as it is in Stephen's performance in the library. If Stephen's interpretation is no more than a making over of the plays in light of his personal concerns, it seems more interesting as a creative act than as a critical act.

But the distinction between creative and critical acts may not be as easy to make in the case of Joyce as some would like it to be. Joyce differs from his contemporaries Pound and Eliot in that he has not left behind a substantial body of criticism as distinguished from his poetry, drama, and fiction. To be sure, there is a collection of his critical writings, but it includes essays written, for the most part, early in his career, none of which had the effect of shaping critical opinion that the critical essays of Pound and Eliot had. What happens with Joyce is that once he starts writing fiction he starts to include his criticism within his art. Even those favorite terms of Joycean critics, "epiphany" and "classical" temper, occur in *Stephen Hero*. The fact that, after abandoning the adolescent work in which these two terms occur, Joyce seems to have rarely used them might be a fitting comment on Joyce's attitude toward these terms, which Goldberg and others find essential for an understanding of Joyce's "mature" aesthetics. Perhaps he stopped using the terms for a good reason. Yet such speculation aside, suffice it to say that one implication of Joyce's move to include his theorizing within his art is that, for Joyce, criticism and art quite literally merge. Thus, it is not surprising to find Joyce's influence on today's debate about critical theory coming not from critics reading his essays but indirectly through figures such as Jacques Derrida. Nor is it surprising that the Shakespeare theory Joyce once had as his own and then passes to his fictional character anticipates in many ways the theory of literature developed by Harold Bloom.[9]

Joyce's relationship to Shakespeare seems a perfect example of what Bloom would call the anxiety of influence. That Joyce had a self-conscious rivalry with Shakespeare is easy to document. Nora Joyce once remarked to a friend, "There's only one man he has to beat now, and that's that Shakespeare."[10] For an artist intent on trying to create something new in a world in which there is nothing new under the sun, Shakespeare is the man to worry about. He is the artist who comes closest to competing with God and his creation of the world. "After God Shakespeare has created most" (*U* 212.41). Thus, in *Ulysses*, Joyce sets out to become one of the "young Irish bards" John Eglinton hopes will "create a figure which the world will set beside Saxon Shakespeare's Hamlet" (*U* 185.7, 8–9).

9. Harold Bloom, *The Anxiety of Influence* (New York: Oxford University Press, 1973). I admit my anxiety over misreading Mr. Bloom.
10. Richard Ellmann, *Ulysses on the Liffey* (New York: Oxford University Press, 1972), 81.

Viewed in Bloom's terms, the interpretation of Shakespeare that Joyce gives to Stephen would admittedly be subjective, but then the history of poetry and criticism is a record of similarly powerfully subjective misreadings. By misreading a strong poet who comes before him, the poet-critic tries to escape the controlling influence of the "father" by clearing out a new creative space for himself, thus engendering the continuation of poetry. Nonetheless, the context in which Joyce places his theory makes it defy Bloom's categories in a number of ways. In so doing, it raises questions about the subjective poetics that Bloom advocates, while still accounting for the subject in the act of interpretation. But first let us look at the similarities along with some objections that could be raised about the truth of Stephen's theory.

To create the figure "the world will set beside Saxon Shakespeare's Hamlet," Joyce creates Stephen. As a way of revenging himself upon the doom of repetition that time imposes, Joyce has his Hamlet re-create Shakespeare's life from a Joycean perspective. Although Joyce follows Shakespeare in historical time and is, therefore, doomed to repeat to a certain extent what his predecessor has created, in his constructing a critical account of Shakespeare's life Joyce can make his Shakespeare repeat aspects of his own life. Not content with this ascendancy, Joyce includes Shakespeare within the pages of his own work, gains control over him, and reduces him to a babbling syphilitic. Through the act of writing, Joyce usurps Shakespeare's priority in historical time by bringing Shakespeare under his control in narrative time. But Joyce has still not established his superiority. The mere fact that he is compelled to rival Shakespeare acknowledges Joyce's debt to him and reestablishes Shakespeare's priority in time. Just as Stephen, born into a colonial English-speaking country, has been deprived of his authority to speak originally, so Joyce, born after Shakespeare, has had taken from him his authority to create originally.[11] Joyce's very means of outdoing Shakespeare remind him that Shakespeare came first. Joyce cannot reverse all-powerful time, which has

11. See Edward Said, "Contemporary Fiction and Criticism," *Tri Quarterly*, No. 33 (Spring, 1975), *Ongoing American Fiction*, 247–50, for a discussion of Joyce as a colonial writer.

dictated that Joyce must follow Shakespeare in history. Joyce's Hamlet will always be a repetition of Shakespeare's Hamlet.

The sense of revenge and outdoing that Stephen describes in Shakespeare's life and art is reflected in his own performance. As both Buck and Stephen know, one purpose of Stephen's performance is to get the better of Englishman Haines. The problem is, however, that when the agreed-upon hour for Haines to be dazzled by a display of Irish wit arrives, Haines does not. He is off buying Hyde's *Love Songs of Connacht*. Haines's failure to appear at the performance that will put him in his place recalls the after-dinner speech in "The Dead," when Gabriel plans to use the occasion to revenge himself on Miss Ivors and then finds that Miss Ivors has left. The object of revenge too often disappears or is absent.

Nonetheless, provided with an audience, no matter how small, willing to listen to his display of midsummer's madness, Stephen cannot hold his tongue. That tongue, unbound by the sacred spirits of Ireland, alcohol, does not wait for a tardy Englishman. Stephen can so easily deliver his symposium to an audience lacking its principal member because his performance is not the spontaneous display of genius he makes it out to be. It is a set-piece performance. Buck, for one, has heard it before. He has warned Eglinton to expect paradoxes, and that morning he helps publicize it to Haines: "It's quite simple. He proves by algebra that Hamlet's grandson is Shakespeare's grandfather and that he himself is the ghost of his own father" (*U* 18.10–12). Then Buck joins the library discussion midway without missing the thread of Stephen's argument. "You were speaking of the gaseous vertebrate, if I mistake not?" (*U* 197.22–23).

As a staged set piece, Stephen's delivery of his theory takes on the characteristics of a performative utterance. Its aim seems to be to rival while entertaining, not to reveal the truth. In this respect it is similar to a number of critics' views of *Ulysses*. *Ulysses*, they argue, should be read for the pleasure it provides, not the truth it reveals. Indeed, motivated by vanity, revenge, and Jameson's, Stephen's theory is certainly hard to take seriously. Stephen himself destroys his own credibility when Eglinton asks him, "Do you believe your own theory?" and he promptly replies, "No" (*U* 213.42–214.1). But Stephen leaves his belief in question by quoting the Bible, "I believe, O Lord, help my unbelief" (*U* 214.15). It may be that understanding and play are connected more closely than we think.

Just as we find ourselves learning from *Ulysses* even though the motives behind writing it may not have been pure, so Stephen learns from his theory. The difference is that we learn while being entertained; Stephen learns while entertaining. Although we are clearly reminded that Stephen has delivered his talk before, we also get the sense that there is something special about this particular repetition. In the act of repeating himself to this particular audience Stephen seems to come up with a genuine insight. Although infinitely repeatable, Stephen's performance, in new circumstances and with new audiences, can yield new insights or at least a repetition of old ones. In this way Stephen's performance is like any literary text, including the plays he is interpreting. Shakespeare's plays too are infinitely repeatable but continue to engage their audiences in new understandings. Most particularly in this respect, Stephen's performance is like the book in which it occurs. On the one hand, there is nothing special about what happens in *Ulysses*. Its actions could be repeated any day in Dublin. On the other hand, there is something special about this particular repetition of the Dublin commonplace. In the case of the "now, the here" of Stephen's performance, if his audience does not include the expected Englishman, it does include an Irish audience just as appropriate.

Having missed the opportunity to outdo a member of the conquering race, Stephen must be content with rivaling his small Irish audience, just as Joyce, while perhaps not matching Shakespeare, does outdo countryman Yeats. At the end of the chapter, Buck asks Stephen, "Couldn't you do the Yeats touch?" (*U* 216.23–24) and then misquotes Yeats's comment on Lady Gregory's work: "The most beautiful book that has come out of our country in my time. One thinks of Homer" (*U* 216.27–28). Joyce will really try to make Ireland think of Homer. But as the reaction to *Dubliners* and *A Portrait* already foretold, Joyce's Irish audience would never appreciate his or Stephen's wit. Instead of seeing him as participating in a larger tradition, they try to tie him to his Irish predecessors. Appropriately, in the library Best insists on mentioning "another Irish commentator, Mr George Bernard Shaw"

(*U* 196.6–7) and considers Wilde's paradoxes "the most brilliant of all" (*U* 198.29). Such comments only add to the insult Stephen has previously received, being snubbed by his audience of the "cultic twalette." Colum, George Roberts, and Miss Mitchell are included in A.E.'s collection *New Songs: A Lyric Selection*, but not Stephen. It could be argued that only by repeating his theory for this particular audience does Stephen start to understand its themes of revenge and outdoing.

> What the hell are you driving at?
> I know. Shut up. Blast you! I have reasons.
> *Amplius. Adhuc. Iterum. Postea.*
> Are you condemned to do this? (*U* 207.31–34)

Interpretation need not be a making over of a text in light of the interpreter's prejudices, it can also be that encounter that reveals the interpreter's prejudices to himself. It is the way in which Stephen's act of understanding grows out of the specific situation of delivering an old performance to a new audience that starts to distinguish his theory from the categories set up by Harold Bloom.

Bloom's theory of the anxiety of influence works for poets in a limited time span. Bloom charts his map of misreading according to the poets he has studied most closely, the Romantics. His theory depends on the historical consciousness he has inherited from them. It was the Romantics who posited the radical otherness of the past. Linked to a belief in the radical otherness of the past is the Romantics' desire for originality. If the past is other, the present must always be new; thus, the present is in constant rivalry with the past.

But the Romantics' view of history is not shared by all poets. For example, Bloom's theory does not work for pre-Romantic poets such as Jonson and Donne, who have a very different sense of the past. Certainly Jonson's Celia poems, which attempt to rewrite Catullus' "Vivamus, mea Lesbia" in the vernacular, or Donne's rewriting of lines from Propertius to start "The Sun Rising" are not products of an anxiety of influence. Similarly, Bloom's theory does not work for Joyce, who does not share the Romantics' historical consciousness. He does not, as Hugh Kenner explains, "because the sheer otherness of the past was a Romantic invention, and Romanticism skipped Ireland. Unless the past is other, your relationship can never be one of continuity, nor yet of discontinuity: only identity, with costumes altered. So Stephen has Shakespeare trudging to London whistling *The girl I left behind me* [*U* 191.1], and asserts that 'his pageants, the histories, sail fullbellied on a tide of Mafeking enthusiasm' [*U* 205.3–4]: the Armada an episode in a seventeenth-century Boer War."[12]

To claim that Romanticism skipped Ireland may be to overstate the case, but Romanticism did arrive late in Ireland and had a much shorter life. It is, in fact, representatives of Ireland's version of Romanticism who make up Stephen's audience in the library. His rejection of their point of view signals Stephen's attempt to work out a different relation to the past from the one that John Eglinton puts forth. "History shows that to be true, *inquit Eglintonus Chronolologos*. The ages succeed one another" (*U* 206.29–30). Rather than affirming the notion of an apostolic succession founded on the mystical estate of fatherhood, Stephen exposes it as a possible legal fiction. By showing Stephen in the process of delivering his theory, Joyce does just the opposite of repressing the anxiety that results from his inability to eliminate the priority "father" Shakespeare has over him. In giving Shakespeare a special chapter in his book, Joyce readily acknowledges his influence. Just as Bloom's theory does not work for pre-Romantic writers, neither does it work for those post-Romantic writers, like Joyce, who are as aware as Bloom is of their anxiety about being influenced (which is not to say that Joyce does not have other areas of repression). Joyce, as do other contemporary writers influenced by him, acknowledges his debt to the past not by repressing it but by self-consciously rewriting those texts he finds most worthy of rereading—the myth of Daedalus, the Bible, the *Odyssey*.

By placing his interpretation of Shakespeare within a fictional work, Joyce creates a situation in which we, much like Stephen, can believe and disbelieve his theory. In one sense, he has disowned his theory. It no longer has authorial authority because it has been given to a character whose authority to speak truthfully is continually undercut. As part of the larger fiction of *Ulysses*, the Shakespeare theory is self-consciously acknowledged to consist of more fiction than fact. Stephen, you will

12. Hugh Kenner, *Joyce's Voices* (Berkeley: University of California Press, 1978), 49–50.

remember, reminds himself and the reader of his anachronisms. Yet it is one of the characteristics of both the larger fiction in which it appears and the theory itself to call attention to the fictional nature of the distinction between fact and fiction, criticism and art, subject and object. There is not one interpretation of Shakespeare that is "fact," making all others "fiction," not one correct reading and countless misreadings. Instead, interpretation itself is temporal, always moving with the times. By giving Stephen a theory he once had, Joyce emphasizes the temporal nature of understanding. In one sense the theory has been cast off, rejected. Preserved in the pages of *Ulysses* so that it can be seen in retrospective arrangement, it has all the qualities of a period piece. On the other hand, dated as it may seem, the theory allows us to see that interpretation is always the result of a specific situation and that understanding can result from an encounter with the text in that situation.

It is the failure to account for the specific temporal nature of understanding that curiously enough aligns someone like Harold Bloom with his "objective" enemies who call his theory of interpretation subjective. As is often argued, Bloom's use of the term *misreading* implies the existence of a correct reading. Thus, a misreading inevitably seems to be a distortion of a true understanding of a work. What Bloom has done, however, is trap himself in a dilemma similar to Nietzsche's in "The Use and Abuse of History."[13] Like Nietzsche, Bloom admits the impossibility of an objective understanding of the past; caught in the Romantics' belief in the otherness of the past, he holds out for the knowledge of an inaccessible past as an ideal. If one adopts a different view of the past, this dilemma does not exist, and the charge of subjectivity needs to be reconsidered.

To posit the radical otherness of the past is to posit a present self free to make over the past on its own terms. But the critic's self is not an autonomous entity free to assert its will independently. Instead, the self is always immersed in circumstances that shape its identity. Self-understanding comes in an attempt to understand those shaping cir-

13. See David Couzens Hoy, *The Critical Circle* (Berkeley: University of California Press, 1978), 133–41.

cumstances. Those circumstances, in turn, are understood in light of the self they have shaped. The self is not a static entity but a being in time. "But I, entelechy, form of forms, am I by memory because under everchanging forms" (*U* 189.39–40).

It is significant that, for Stephen, memory gives his I its I-ness—memory, even if flawed, is the mother of the Muses. It is memory that allows the writing of poetry and history and it is memory that is vital to self-understanding. Self-understanding involves understanding selves from the past. As Stephen remarks, "That which I was is that which I am and that which in possibility I may come to be. So in the future, the sister of the past, I may see myself as I sit here now but by reflection from that which then I shall be" (*U* 194.30–34). Woven together from quotations echoing A.E., Pater, and Shelley, Stephen's passage acknowledges its debt to Romanticism while groping for a more complete relationship to the past. Understanding the past, whether it be the world of Shakespeare's plays or a past self, always involves an act of interpretation from the standpoint of the present. Yet that present self is in turn a product of the past. The critic acts and is acted on.

A reader's encounter with a text resulting in understanding is not a case of the reader's adopting a stance of objectivity so that his reading mirrors a preconstituted meaning within the text. Nor is it a case of the reader's using the text as a mirror to reflect an image of his own subjectivity. Instead, it is that mirror-within-a-mirror process by which the reader is interpreted by the text while the text is interpreted by the reader.

While Stephen's interpretation appears subjective to those locked within the Romantics' sense of the past, it is not as subjective as it seems. This is because the self doing the interpreting comes into existence as a result of attempting to understand those aspects of a living tradition that, existing prior to the self, have shaped the self. In *A Portrait*, Stephen learns of his destiny by trying to understand the meaning of the name he has inherited from the past. In *Ulysses* he gains part of his identity by playing the role of Hamlet, the alter ego of the very Shakespeare he could be accused of making over in his own image. Although, as Kenner points out, he gives Shakespeare the language of the present, he adopts Shakespeare's language to think about Shakespeare and himself.

> How now, sirrah, that pound he lent you when you were hungry?
> Marry, I wanted it.
> Take thou this noble.
> Go to! You spent most of it in Georgina Johnson's bed, clergyman's daughter. Agenbite of inwit. (*U* 189.22–27)

Through dramatizing Stephen's act of interpretation in the library, Joyce offers us a literary history that is a series not of misreadings but of readings and rereadings. To be sure, those readings are by necessity partial. But the recognition of the inevitability of partiality need not lead us either to celebration or to despair. The recognition of our partialness is always a humbling experience, and yet it is exactly this recognition that opens us to a world and time beyond ourselves. The past is not other; it lives in the present. *Ulysses* is not a misreading of the *Odyssey* but a translation better in its own way than any attempt to "restore the original."

The nature of understanding dramatized by Stephen's performance in the library (at least as I have interpreted it) shares important similarities with the theory of hermeneutics developed by Hans-Georg Gadamer. In his book *Truth and Method*, Gadamer places himself in the tradition of phenomenological inquiry, from Husserl to Heidegger, in addition to finding roots, as does Stephen, in Aristotle. What he tries to do is clarify the act of interpretation by describing the process in which understanding takes place rather than prescribing a method to follow.

Gadamer would appreciate Joyce's insistence on placing Stephen's act of interpretation within a dramatic situation; for Gadamer, understanding is always rooted in a situation. Understanding does not merely repeat the past; it participates in present meaning, just as Stephen reconstructs Shakespeare's world in light of his present perspective and Joyce interprets the *Odyssey* by rewriting it in twentieth-century Dublin. To those who argue that such a view of understanding opens interpretation to the whims of subjectivity and rules out the possibility of a true understanding of the past, Gadamer responds that to ignore the interpreter's historical situation is to be not more but less objective, not more but less historical. The interpreter's situatedness (*Situationsgebundenheit*) does not close him off to the past but opens it to him, since it is his particular situation that places him in the flow of time. Thus, the conditions of the interpreter's particular situation are not factors to be eliminated before understanding can take place. They are necessary, making understanding possible. When understanding takes place, rather than a making over of the past or text in light of the interpreter's presuppositions, we have a dialogue in which the interpreter's presuppositions are unsilenced. For Gadamer, understanding includes both increased self-understanding and understanding of the text to be interpreted. In interpreting a text from the past, the interpreter increases his self-understanding by being made aware of the temporal component of his being. The understanding of the text that results from this fusion of the interpreter's horizon with the text's is not a subjective one, "not mine nor my author's but common." In other words, understanding involves, not a mysterious communion of the critic's mind with the author's mind, but participation in shared meaning. What allows that meaning to be shared—and this links Gadamer even more closely with Joyce—is the universal medium in which understanding takes place: language. For Gadamer, as for Joyce, "the relation between language and understanding is seen primarily in the fact that it is the nature of tradition to exist in the medium of language."[14]

By designating language as the medium in which understanding takes place, Gadamer avoids the subject-object dualism on which most theories of hermeneutics stumble. The critic never makes the text totally over in his own image because his understanding must take place in the realm of the text's language. On the other hand, the text is dependent on the critic-reader to bring its language alive. In a similar manner, Gadamer's theory avoids the problems raised by the Romantics' sense of historical otherness. This view of the past can lead to a sort of museum in which the various eras of history are put on display

14. Hans-Georg Gadamer, *Truth and Method*, trans. Garrett Barden and John Cumming (New York: Seabury Press, 1975), 350, 351. Hoy, *The Critical Circle*, is an excellent introduction to Gadamer's work, for the English-speaking reader.

as something to be contemplated. But so long as the past lives and lives in language, we do not need to worry about recapturing it. It is always speaking to us, telling us something about our present. We only have to learn to listen to it, something that *Ulysses'* language more than most makes us do.

Ulysses is not haunted by voices from the past in the same way *The Waste Land* is. The ghosts of *Ulysses* are alive, having returned to walk the streets of twentieth-century Dublin. Similarly, in his Shakespeare theory Stephen offers us a living, not a museum, Shakespeare. It seems no accident that this chapter follows Bloom's escape into a museum, where he tries to hide from his present situation. The task of criticism is not to offer an escape into a museum past; it is to keep the work of art alive. This is what Stephen does in the library. With "coffined thoughts around me, in mummycases, embalmed in spice of words" (*U* 193.37–38), he breathes life once again into Shakespeare's text. "And I heard the voice of that Egyptian highpriest" (*U* 193.39) indicates that Stephen's thoughts turn to Professor MacHugh's rendition of John F. Taylor's speech in "Aeolus." This is appropriate because MacHugh's giving voice to Taylor's speech, which describes how God's sacred word was preserved in "*the tables of the law, graven in the language of the outlaw*" (*U* 143.15–16), is a perfect example of the reader's role in keeping the words of a text alive.

My odyssey will end with my turning to MacHugh's repetition of Taylor's speech, which allows me to speculate on how one very important reader and rereader of *Ulysses* read this passage in a new context and used it to create new potential meanings without altering the words as written. The reader is Joyce, and the rereading takes place after *Ulysses* has been published, if not finished and abandoned.

One of Joyce's most loyal readers, the one who provided him with a printing press to keep his written voice alive—Sylvia Beach—also wanted to keep Joyce's spoken voice alive. She convinced Joyce to record part of *Ulysses* in his own voice. The recording, privately financed by Beach, took place in Paris at the company of, appropriately enough, His Master's Voice. (In "Circe" the M'Intosh-like ghost of Paddy Dignam—resurrected from a dogsbody to a human spirit when his "*dachshund coat becomes a brown mortuary habit*" [*U* 472.17]—

claims to recognize the voice of John O'Connell blaring through a megaphone as "my masters' voice!" [*U* 474.6]. Here is Beach's description of the recording:

Joyce had chosen the speech from the "Aeolus" episode, the only passage that could be lifted out of *Ulysses*, he said, and the only one that was "declamatory" and therefore suitable for recital. He had made up his mind, he told me, that this would be his only reading from *Ulysses*.

I have an idea that it was not for declamatory reasons alone that he chose this passage from "Aeolus." I believe that it expressed something he wanted said and preserved in his own voice. As it rings out—"he lifted his voice above it boldly"—it is more, one feels, than mere oratory.[15]

While Beach's account confirms that Joyce was acutely aware of which parts of *Ulysses* were suitable to be given oral voice, there is some evidence that he was considering another passage. In a letter to Victor Larbaud, 20 November 1924, he writes, "I am not free till the 28 as on the 27 I have to read part of the Sirens for a gramophone record" (*Letters*, *III* III).[16] This comment can be interpreted in a number of ways. It could of course be a mistake. On the other hand, the selection makes sense, given the "oral" character of "Sirens" and his choice of parts of it to be read out loud at an earlier séance to publicize the book in Paris. So sometime btween 20 November and 27 November, Joyce might have reread "Aêolus" and discovered something about the Taylor speech that made it more appropriate.

It is worth looking at the "Aeolus" selection to see if, as Beach suspects, there are reasons other than declamatory ones for Joyce to

15. Sylvia Beach, *Shakespeare and Co.* (New York: Harcourt, Brace, 1956), 170–71.

16. This letter raises another problem—the dating of the recording. It rules out the date of 1923 listed in Alan Parker, *James Joyce: A Bibliography of His Writings, Critical Material, and Miscellanea* (Boston: F. W. Faxon, 1948), 253, a date repeated by Robert H. Demming, *A Bibliography of James Joyce Studies* (2nd ed.; Boston: G. K. Hall, 1977), 112, item 2734. Relying on this letter, Ellmann lists the date of the recording as 1924. But because, as Beach reports, the first recording was a failure, the date of 17 November 1926, listed by John F. Slocum and Herbert Cahoon, *A Bibliography of James Joyce* (London: Rupert Hart-Davis, 1957), 173, may be more accurate. Yet a two-year delay seems unlikely. Perhaps the later date is the date the record was issued to Beach. Furthermore, Joyce might enjoy the fact that Parker mistakenly lists the recording as "O'Molloy's Speech" rather than MacHugh's. Demming again repeats the error.

have chosen this passage as the one to be recorded in his master's voice. It may not be accidental that Joyce's recording, which turns silent print into voice, is of part of "Aeolus," the chapter giving the reader a first-hand account of how Dublin's voices get confined to the silence of print.

The passage (*U* 142.4–143.17) records Professor MacHugh's recitation of John F. Taylor's famous speech comparing the Irish to the people of Israel. Beginning appropriately, "He began," the section employs a typical Joycean strategy. Rather than hearing his master's voice directly, we have a record of Joyce's voice doing what it does best—mimicking other voices. Joyce's voice comes to us masked by the voice of one of his fictional characters adopting the persona of John F. Taylor. Furthermore, the interplay between written and spoken language is typically Joycean. While we normally think of a writer's text as a way of keeping his voice alive, in Joyce's record the author's voice is used to keep part of his text alive. In the record Joyce gives voice to a part of *Ulysses* that records a fictional character supposedly delivering an oral rendition of a speech he reconstructs from memory without the aid of written notes. Similarly, if we can trust the fictional Professor MacHugh, Taylor's original speech was delivered "impromptu" without the aid of notes, for "there was not even one shorthand-writer in the hall" (*U* 141.28–29). If this is true, then the writers who recorded the speech in the 25 October 1901 *Freeman's Journal*, and in the 1903 pamphlet *The Language of the Outlaw*, must have relied on their memories to give us the two written versions of the speech from which Joyce seems to have reconstructed it for us in *Ulysses*. An impromptu speech, recorded in print by memory, reconstructed in a fictional text, where it masquerades as the impromptu oral re-creation of the speech from memory, is finally recorded by a gramophone. The entire situation would be further complicated if, as Ellmann assumes (*JJ* 94–95), Joyce himself was present at Taylor's speech.

The passage is a nice example of the complicated process by which a voice is kept alive to speak to the future. Indeed, as we, the audience, listen to Joyce's recording we feel as though we *"had been transported into a country far away from this country"* (*U* 142.8–9)—and not only from Taylor's Ireland to Egypt but also from where we sit now to a Dublin room on 24 October 1901 to listen to Taylor delivering his speech, or, more accurately, to Joyce's Dublin, 16 June 1904, to listen to MacHugh re-create Taylor's speech. Once we are transported to Joyce's Dublin, we of course journey to the Greece of Homer and, following Stephen's allusion *"and let our crooked smokes"* (U 142.13– 14), to the England of Shakespeare (or is it the England of Cymbeline?). The recording speaks to us now and always. By making all times one, Joyce speaks to each generation: present, past, and future. Each reader-listener feels, *"I heard his words and their meaning was revealed to me"* (U 142.18–19).

This sentence, which is supposedly Taylor's, uttered in response to the previous speaker, also anticipates the end of Taylor's speech, which refers to Moses receiving the Word of God on Mount Sinai. Taylor's allusion to the famous incident in Exodus, in which Moses ascends Mount Sinai to speak with God, makes the way in which the written word and the spoken word interact to keep a voice alive a reflection not only of the circumstances in which Joyce records the passage but also of the subject matter of the passage he chooses. As a chosen member of a chosen race, Moses has the privilege of hearing God's voice directly. While the rest of the people of Israel are denied this immediate revelation, God makes certain that they will "hear" his voice by preserving it in the stone tablets that he places in Moses' hands. Moses' role, then, is much like that of author Joyce in his role as a recorder of Dublin's voices: he acts as the intermediary through which the now silent original voice is preserved in writing to be heard by others. But Moses' role is also like that of the reader, for it is Moses who, although himself not an eloquent man, keeps the voice of the author / God alive by *"bearing in his arms the tables of the law, graven in the language of the outlaw"* (U 143.15–16). It will be Moses who speaks God's Word with his own voice. All this occurs of course in the section entitled "From the Fathers," a "headline" conspicuous by its absence from Joyce's recording. So with his re-creation of MacHugh's re-creation of Taylor's speech completed, Joyce is ready to end the one passage he felt was suitable for his spoken voice. He does so as appropriately as he began. With the confident knowledge that his voice has been heard by the privileged few who have access to his recording, and by the many more who have access to his printed text, Joyce concludes, "He ceased and looked at them, enjoying silence" (*U* 143.17). Joyce can enjoy his silence because even though his spoken voice may be "gone with the wind" (*U* 143.28), his "words howled and scattered to the four winds" (*U* 143.29–30), leaving only "dead noise" (*U* 143.31). Joyce has left behind a text that is like the "Akasic records of all that ever anywhere wherever was" (*U* 143.31-32).

The world of *Ulysses* is so inclusive because through the tale of the telling Joyce invites the reader, no matter how limited and prone to error he might be, to become his accomplice and to participate in the book's creation. "When one reads these strange pages of one long gone one feels that one is at one with one who once" (*U* 40.38–39). Each reader enters into *Ulysses* as he actively interweaves his world with the words of the text, and each reader's world is expanded as he passively submits to the polytropic, turning nature of the book's language, a language that shapes him much as it shapes the book's characters. Invited by that language to make many happy returns to the book's pages, reader after reader participates in an ongoing process that makes *Ulysses* truly a "world without end" (*U* 37.32).

Index